FORM AND FREEDOM

WHAT THE NEW TESTAMENT TEACHES ABOUT CHURCH GOVERNMENT AND CHURCH LEADERSHIP

JEFF BROWN

Bibliographic information published by Die Deutsche Bibliothek
Die Deutsche Bibliothek lists this publication in the Deutsche National-
bibliografie; detailed bibliographic data are available in the Internet at
http://dnb.ddb.de.

ISBN 3-937965-06-8

© 2004 by Jeff Brown
2nd edition

All rights reserved. No part of this book may be reproduced in any form
or by any means without permission in writing from the publisher,
VTR Publications, Gogolstr. 33, 90475 Nürnberg, Germany,
vtr@compuserve.com, http://www.vtr-online.de.

Unless otherwise stated, scripture quotations are taken from the
New American Standard Bible.

Cover illustration: VTR

Printed in the UK by Lightning Source

TABLE OF CONTENTS

DEDICATION	5
ACKNOWLEDGEMENTS	7
FOREWORD by Douglas R. McLachlan	9
WHY THIS BOOK HAS BEEN WRITTEN	13

CHAPTER 1:
A DEFENSE OF SELF-GOVERNMENT FOR THE CHURCH 15

   Arguments: 18
      1. Christ is the Only Head of the Church
         (Eph. 5:23; Col. 1:18) 18
      2. The Self-Government of the Local Church is a
         Biblical Principle 19
      3. The Greek Word for "Church" Connotes the
         Idea of Self-Government 21
      4. Examples of Self-Government from the
         New Testament 26
   Effects of the Self-Government of the Church 35
   Why Do Some Find the Self-Government of the
      Local Church a False Principle? 38
   Recommended for Further Study 45

CHAPTER 2:
MAKING THE SELF-GOVERNMENT OF
THE LOCAL CHURCH FUNCTION WELL 57

   Individual Voice 57
   Individual Responsibility 59
   Strong Leadership 60
   The Inspired Scriptures 61
   Good Organization 64
   Encouragement of the Use of Spiritual Gifts 68
   Unity 70
   Prayer 72
   Grace and Forgiveness 73
   Recommended for Further Study 74

CHAPTER 3:
ELDERS AND THEIR WORK 79
Terms for Church Leaders 79
The Three Terms Describe One Person 82
Qualifications for the Office 84
Must Elders Be Multiple Or May They Be Single in
  a Congregation? 85
Is the Election of Pastors/Elders by the
  Congregation a Biblical Procedure? 89
Bishops, in the New Testament Sense, Are Local,
  Not Regional in Their Jurisdiction 93
The Work of Pastoring, Considered from the
  Biblical Perspective 101
Recommended for Further Study 108

CHAPTER 4:
DEACONS AND THEIR MINISTRY 120
The Meaning of the Word "Deacon" 121
The Place of the Deacon in the New Testament 122
Personal Requirements for the Deacon 124
The Exercise of the Ministry of Deacon 128
Training 129
Recommended Resources 130

CONCLUSION 134

BIBLIOGRAPHY 136

APPENDIX 1:
Development of Episcopacy in the First Five Centuries 149

APPENDIX 2:
**Twenty-One Questions for Spiritual Leaders from
1 Timothy 3:1-7; Titus 1:5-9** 150

APPENDIX 3:
**A Partial List of Church Groups in the United States
That Practice Local Church Self Government
(Congregationalism)** 152

Dedication

The work and thinking of preachers is molded by others whose lives and teaching have left their imprint upon them. My thinking has on this subject been highly influenced by many, more than I can list. With this in mind, this book is affectionately dedicated to the following men who most affected my thinking and my heart on this matter:

Rolland D. McCune, my theology professor.

Collins Glenn, my pastor for many, many years.

Paul Fosmark, my mentor in Christian leadership

Acknowledgements

After I had completed about one fourth of this book, I picked up a copy of Dr. Earl Radmacher's *The Nature of the Church* and read it. Many concepts presented in his book contributed significantly to my forming thoughts for portions of *Form and Freedom*. When I had completed the rough draft, I sent him a copy, which he graciously assented to read and comment on. As would be expected, we do not agree in every point, but Dr. Radmacher was convinced that my book would function well as a companion volume to his book on the Church. He also shared ideas, corrections and encouragements as he read the manuscript, that were especially helpful. I would also like to thank Dr. Kevin Bauder and Dr. William Smallman for reading the manuscript through and making many useful suggestions. Likewise I would like to thank two former classmates, Dr. Mike Windsor, for helping gather resources in the early phase of the writing and Dr. Roy Beacham for helping get the project done. Thanks also goes to my niece, Kathy Todd, my wife, Linda and our longtime friend, Linda Russell, who read and corrected the entire text and helped turn it into a good one. It would not be right for me to overlook the president of Baptist Mid-Missions, Dr. Gary Anderson, whose able leadership and sensitivities to church polity and teamwork have been a tremendous asset to all of us associated with the mission. Though nowhere quoted his outlook pervades much of what is written here. Finally, I would like to mention my co-worker, Burdette Bergen, without whose gentle nudges to get me to do this, the book would never have been started. Thanks Burdette.

Foreword

by Douglas R. McLachlan

It is undeniably true that God loves His church for "He purchased it with His own blood." (Acts 20:28 NKJV) This can only mean that the church belongs exclusively to God Himself by right of redemption, and "the purchase price was nothing less than the life-blood of His beloved Son."[1] No stronger affirmation of God's love for His church could be imagined.

If God loves His church, Christians should too. For all authentic believers in Jesus, the church is the body we celebrate. And celebration is a component of life which by and large is conspicuous by its absence on most of planet earth. Michael Medved said in *Imprimus* several years ago that the number one service requested at the medical clinics on the campuses of the prestigious Ivy League universities on the east coast of America by the privileged and often pampered students who attend them is help for depression. Celebration and joy are conspicuous by their absence in our fallen world.

Authentic celebration or joy is sourced, first, in God and His redemptive work in our behalf. The recipients of that rescue operation have great reason to celebrate. But it is found, second, in the communities of faith, those authentic biblical churches, which Christ left on planet earth to carry out His work. As Luke records of that prototypical model of the New Testament church in Acts 2, "...they ate their food with gladness and simplicity of heart, praising God and having favor with all the people..." (vv 46, 47 NKJV).

What is it that people find in Christ's church that makes it such a celebrative environment? 1 Timothy 3:15 is a classic text, at the very heart of Paul's epistle on local church doctrine and decorum, which supplies us with the answer. When Paul thinks of the church, he thinks in terms of *three graphic pictures*, each of which provides a reason to celebrate it.

First, he celebrates family because the church is "the *house(hold) of God.*" With the disintegration of family in western civilization, people need the kind of caring familial community that can only be found in the church of Jesus Christ.

Second, he celebrates life because the church is "the church of the *living God.*" All through Scripture God is always defined as the living God, and always in contrast to the lifeless and useless idols which plague every generation in every culture. And Christian conversion is defined by Paul as nothing less than turning "to God from idols to serve the living and true God" (1 Thessalonians 1:9 NKJV). In Scripture conversion to Christ was always followed by incorporation into the local assembly: "And the Lord added to the church daily those who were being saved" (Acts 2:47 NKJV). There is something wonderfully celebrative about the living God imparting spiritual life to the living dead (Ephesians 2:1), and then joining them to the life-base, the habitat or dwelling place of the living God (Ephesians 2:19-22). In a world suffused with death, access to such life resonates joyfully with our hearts.

Third, he celebrates truth because the church is "the pillar and ground of *the truth.*" Not only is the church a home-base for the alienated and disenfranchised, and a life-base for the spiritually dead, it is a truth-base for those who are deceived. All of us are children of deception since all are children of Adam and Eve who were deceived by Satan in the Garden of Eden. What we need more than all else is access to the truth, and God has ordained that New Testament local churches are to be "the pillar and ground" (the protectors and proclaimers) of His truth. What makes God's truth so essential to our journey is the incredible impact it makes on human beings who believe it. Truth is regenerational (James 1:18); liberational (John 8:32); and transformational (John 17:17). And nothing so suffuses the human experience with joy as a dynamic experience of regeneration, liberation and transformation. For the local church to be a truth-dispensing agency of this sort is both a sobering responsibility and an awesome privilege.

Family, life and truth – these are the rich resources which become available to humankind through the dynamic body-life and missional heartbeat of God's church. Without doubt this spiritual agency is infinitely valuable in terms of its mission and deeply loved by the triune Godhead.

Church planter, Jeff Brown, is eminently qualified to write a book on the governance of the church. Like God Himself, Jeff, too, loves the church. He has labored long and hard to plant a New Testament church in the midst of a thoroughly secular culture; a church that is self-supporting, self-propagating and self-governing. I have had the privilege of speaking to this body of believers in Erlangen, Germany, and it is a thrill to see how God has blessed his and his family's efforts.

A part of the stewardship of the rich ministry of a local assembly of believers is possessing a proper understanding of the Bible's teaching on the subject of church polity or governance. Jeff's careful and thoughtful treatment of this subject deserves the attention of pastors and people who care about the church of Jesus Christ. I gladly commend this rich body of teaching to all who love the church.

Douglas R. McLachlan, Pastor
Fourth Baptist Church, Plymouth, Minnesota

---

[1] F.F. Bruce, *The Book of Acts, Revised* (Grand Rapids: William B. Eerdmans Publishing Company, 1988), 393.

Why This Book Has Been Written

The type of church government one holds to is not necessarily a sign of spirituality or spiritual maturity. Believers who practiced nearly every sort of church government have been mightily used of the Lord through the centuries: John Chrysostom of the ancient church of Constantinople, Peter Waldo of the Waldensian movement, Martin Luther in the Lutheran church, the Wesleys and George Whitefield from the Anglican church, the missions movement of the Moravian church, George Mueller of the Brethren, Charles Spurgeon from the Baptists. Each of these belonged to a church whose organization differed from the others named.

Likewise, church government is not the main theme of the Bible – the meaning of the life, death, and resurrection of Jesus Christ is. So why consider the subject of church government? In the first place, the New Testament deals with the topic on several occasions. That is reason enough. As Christians come together for worship and work, they will have to organize themselves. Secondly, disagreements about church government have been the cause of repeated conflict in Christianity through the centuries. This tendency toward conflict gives Christians all the more reason to take a careful look at what the Scripture says about the subject. A humble study and application of what the New Testament teaches on church order and leadership leads to harmony, not conflict. It is eisegesis and pragmatism, not the Scriptures themselves, that have supplied the environment for church warfare.

No doubt, what is written here will arouse criticism since it contradicts some long-held religious positions. Though there will be much interaction with the proponents of various other systems, the purpose of this writing is not to wrangle. Nor does the author call into question the spiritual character of those with whom he disagrees. Many of those writers, in fact, have had very positive impact on his own ministry. This book is written primarily to clarify the position of congregational church government, essentially for those who already hold that position. Historically, free churches that adopted congregationalism did so as a result of their pursuit of other goals, such as churches composed of believers only. It is the writer's opinion that an open study of the Scripture on this matter will lead one to the conclusion that the government of the church is congregational. It is, however, not the object of this book to proselytize. That much said, if those of other persuasions will deal with what is written here, it would be a healthy thing, to make their own convictions more firm, and hopefully, more biblical.

The New Testament teaches a church government that has both form and freedom: both structure and spontaneity. It asserts rule in the church. It expects activism in the membership. It teaches reverence for the leaders. It commends dialogue in the body. Assertive leadership alongside congregational voice was not designed by the Bible writers to be a tension. Instead the two form a balance.

Church government and church leadership are overlapping themes. Pastoral duties cannot be separated from pastoral ethics. For that reason, the first chapter of this book is a theological-exegetical study, but the second chapter is a practical one, as are parts of chapters three and four. After leaders learn what is to be done they almost inevitably begin to ask, "How?"

Good church decision-making is based as much on maturity and love as it is on proper structure. Woe to the pastor who believes that proper church structure is an answer to all church problems! One of the greatest needs of present day churches is strong, godly leadership. Churches need leaders who will order their lives according to the pattern of Scripture. They need leaders who will ask the question, "What would Jesus do?" even when it means losing everything. The enemies of the orthodox formulation of the Trinity once taunted Athanaisus, "Don't you know that the whole world is against you?" He replied, "Then Athanasius is against the whole world!" In fact, Athanasius was not the only Christian who asserted the truth of the Trinity as we now believe in it. But he was willing, if necessary, to stand only with God for the truth. This ancient example sets a pattern so very necessary for church leadership of every age, especially our own.

Chapter 1

A Defense of Self-Government for the Church

The disintegration of empires during the last half of the 20th century, including the Soviet Empire, has brought about an unprecedented shift toward democracy among nations around the world. The desire that people have for democracy often lies deeper than one would expect. In 1982 in El Salvador, for instance, the western world was astonished by a massive voter turnout of citizens for their first free elections. The media were red-faced, since they had predicted that only a minority would vote, convinced that the common man of El Salvador was in sympathy with the Marxist rebels. Instead, they chose the right-leaning candidates. Democracy is not always successful (its attempt in Russia, for instance), but its worldwide admiration can hardly be questioned. In many cases, its emergence has been intertwined with Christian ideals and Biblical truths. Take the following example of a secular German news reporter about the East German pro-democracy movement, just before the Berlin wall came down,

> At the entrance of the Nicholas Church in the center of Leipzig, one encounters a colorful picture: thick bundles of autumn flowers in brilliant colors lie in front of the doors. Between these stand burning candles. In the middle someone has placed a clearly written note, "It is for freedom that Christ has set us free. Stand firm, then, and do not let yourselves be burdened again by a yoke of bondage." The fading bouquets are meant for those young citizens of Leipzig, who have been jailed in the past weeks, because they spoke out for democracy.[1]

It is a fact that democratic-functioning religious bodies emerged in Germany nearly 500 years ahead of the "New Forum" movement of 1989, and spread throughout Europe.[2] At the time, they were called "Anabaptists" or "Baptists" (the German words were *Wiedertäufer* and *Täufer*, respectively). The Anabaptists held to the principle of the self-governing church. William Estep goes so far as to say that "the congregational principle of church government was born with the Anabaptists of the sixteenth century."[3] They later took various names, including Mennonites, Baptists, Hutterites and Amish. They carried these democratic ideas to America (though the Hutterites and Amish remained outside of the American political process at its inception), and along with the Congregationalists,[4] had a significant impact on the development of democracy in America.[5]

In the 12th century Pierre de Bruys established a type of democratic independent church in southern France. At about the same time, the religious reformer Arnold de Brescia attempted to help reestablish the Roman Senate in Rome and the Pope was forced to flee.[6] In his *Defensor Pacis*, written in 1327, Marsiglio de Padua, court physician of Emperor Louis the Bavarian argued that discipline of heretics lies in the hands of the people of the church, not in the hands of bishops, and that bishops in the New Testament sense are local clergy. He likewise argued that the authority of human princes rests solely on the consent of their citizens.[7] John Wycliff (1330-1384) is best known as a religious reformer ahead of the Reformation, and for his translation of the Bible into English. But he was also an early political thinker.

> Wycliffe propounded the theory of "dominion by grace," according to which each man was God's direct tenant-in-chief, immediately responsible to God, and immediately responsible to obey His law. And by God's law Wycliffe meant not canon law, which he repudiated, but the Bible. The Bible was to him the rule of faith and practice, including ecclesiastical practice, for he did not conceive that the Bible's guidance on questions of church order and organization could be ambiguous.[8]

Indeed, he was held partly responsible for the Peasants' Revolt in 1377.[9] He had taught that the people could legitimately depose corrupt rulers in either the ecclesiastical or civil realm.[10]

The Taborites of Bohemia allowed the laity a role in church life, as well as in political life. The initial form of the Peasants' Revolt in Germany was non-violent, and motivated by the evangelical teachings of Luther. The movement's "Twelve articles," written in early 1525, were modest demands by modern standards. They began with the declaration of the right of each community to choose its own pastor. With this demand, Luther was in full agreement.[11] Fourteen years later the reformer, Martin Bucer, wrote in the Ziegenhagen Ordinance (for the land of Hesse), that church elders were to be chosen by the populace.[12] During the Reformation in England Congregationalists and Baptists espoused the self-government of the local congregation, including the election of pastors and deacons, as their early confessions demonstrate.[13]

In the United States, the Methodists and Baptists were primarily responsible for converting the enslaved blacks living there. Through their contradicting motivations of religious liberty and racism, the white contingent of these two confessions first won, then alienated their black brethren. The black Methodists and Baptists formed their own indigenous denominations.[14] Nathan Hatch says, "By its democratization in black hands, the church served as the major rallying point for human dignity, freedom, and equality among those who bore slavery's cruel yoke."[15]

This historical review is written, not to state that all good evangelicals will also be supporters of political democracy, but to point out that historically, the evangelical faith and democratic ideas were intertwined. From the time of the Mediaeval Evangelicals until the present day, the evangelical faith has recognized the direct access of the believer to Christ, and repudiated other forms of mediation. It has emphasized the equality of believers before Christ, rather than the hierarchy of the Church. Historically, these ideas have inevitably spilled over into the political realm.

Arguments

1. Christ is the Only Head of the Church (Eph. 5:23; Col. 1:18).
No other person or entity is said to be head of the church. The church is, after all, his body. Thus Christ rules each local church, and each Christian is directly under his rule. One of the earliest Congregational statements of faith, The Savoy Confession, presents the argument in the following way:

> By the appointment of the Father, all Power for the Calling, Institution, Order, or Government of the Church is invested in a Supreme and Sovereign manner in the Lord Jesus Christ, as King and Head thereof ... . To each of these churches thus gathered, according unto his mind declared in his Word, he hath given all that Power and Authority which is any way needful for their carrying on that order in Worship and Discipline which he hath instituted for them to observe with Commands and Rules for the due and right exerting and executing of that Power.[16]

Commenting on Colossians 1:18, Arnold notes that, "as head of the church, Christ provides leadership and direction for his people while at the same time is the source of the church's life energy for its growth to maturity."[17] Later, in 2:19, "Paul calls on the Colossians to depend on Christ alone for leadership and for power and strengthening."[18] Leon Morris, an Anglican, states that the direct headship of Christ is a fair Scriptural basis for the position of the self-government of the church.[19]

In addition, Revelation 2 and 3 presents Christ as directly acting and ruling in each of seven local churches in the province of Asia. Earl Radmacher comments, "Each local church is directly responsible to Christ and dependent on Him for leadership and sustenance, even as is the body of Christ in its entirety."[20] J. Theodore Mueller argues,

> There is in these two dynamic chapters no stress whatever on outward church organization as it is being urged in many areas of Christendom today. The seven representative churches of Asia, humanly speaking, were greatly in need of such organization, for they were troubled by spiritual foes in many ways. But

nowhere does the Holy Spirit suggest any group organization of these churches as a means of offense or defense.[21]

This truth leads to two conclusions with respect to church government: first, each church rules itself, since it is directly under Christ. This does not contradict the idea of designated leaders within the church, as the New Testament teaches these as well, and sees no contradiction (note that Paul, who wrote Colossians and Ephesians, said a fair amount about overseers and deacons, e.g. Phil. 1:1 and 1 Tim. 3). But the New Testament does not teach of any bishop, council or synod that has authority over a group of churches. Second, since Christ is the head of the Church (Eph. 5:23), "he is in living, vital contact with each member."[22] Therefore individual members of a local congregation involve themselves in the government of the body.

Kevin Giles is one who feels that the congregational ecclesiology is seriously flawed. It appeals to the modern evangelical mind "because these ideas feel right to the modern mind imbued with the philosophy of individualism . . . ."[23] He says further, "The New Testament is not predicated on such a view of life. Those who suggest this, or base their ecclesiology on this premise, are mistaken – for in the ancient world, communal thinking was pervasive."[24] Giles marshals several strong arguments against the congregational position, some of which will be considered later in this chapter. At this point, it is sufficient to note . . . that the idea of congregational government can be proven at least as far back as Luther. It certainly was not in harmony with the prevailing philosophy and reigning ideas of government at that time. The Anabaptists and the Congregationalists were not motivated by leading philosophies, but by what they perceived as New Testament truths, on which they were willing to stake their lives.

2. *The Self-Government of the Local Church is a Biblical Principle.*

Every believer is a priest (1 Pet. 2:5,9). He receives this spiritual position the moment he receives the new birth. In the Mosaic Law, God designated the line of Aaron for the priesthood of Israel. No Israelite (much less a Gentile) could approach God without going through one of the priests descended from Aaron. But in the New Testament, the believer is given direct access to the Father through Christ, *without* any other intermediary (1 Tim. 2:5). Every Christian has spiritual understanding, to the point that he can interpret the Bible for himself (1 Cor. 2:14-16; 1 Jn. 2:20, 27). Every Christian can approach the throne of God (Eph 2:18; Heb. 4:14-16; 10:19-22).

Eduard Schweizer states,

> All the New Testament Witnesses are sure of one decisive fact: official priesthood, which exists to conciliate and mediate between God and the community, is found in Judaism and paganism; but since Jesus Christ there has been only one such office – that of Jesus Christ himself. It is shared by the whole church and never by one church member as distinct from others.[25]

Dexter formulates this situation in the following way: All church members ". . . come into it upon the same conditions, make the same promises, and seek the same ends. All stand upon an equality before God as to their need of salvation, as to the way of salvation, and as to the duties of salvation."[26]

The obvious conclusion is that all genuine Christians stand on the same spiritual level.[27] During the Reformation, as these truths became widespread, self-governing churches began developing. Wherever such doctrines are widely preached, Christians will also form the conclusion that the church should reflect this truth in a practical way. Not every Christian is called to be a leader or a preacher (the exclusiveness of these roles is taught in 1 Timothy 3:2-7, Titus 1:5-9 and Hebrews 13:17), but every Christian is a priest.[28]

Some assert that the local church is a theocracy.[29] In one sense this is true, as the headship of Christ has been argued in the previous section. But one must also understand that in each instance of a theocracy in the Bible, there was a mediator. In the church, Christ is the mediator (1 Tim. 2:5). No other is mentioned. Christ did not designate viceroys here on earth (if he did, then the Episcopal system – whether Anglican, Roman Catholic, or Eastern Orthodox - is the right system). The issue is not to emphasize the theocratic nature of the local church in order to determine church structure. Rather, it is a matter of learning from the Scriptures how the vice-regents of Christ govern themselves in the local setting on earth, as they acknowledge only one High Priest.

3. The Greek Word for "Church" Connotes the Idea of Self-Government.

The Apostles could have used several different words to denote the Church.[30] The early church historian, Eusebius, in fact, used the word *thiasos* to speak of the church, as did Lucian.[31] Various cult-societies contemporary with the time of the apostles used a variety of Greek words to denote themselves.[32] These words, the apostles studiously avoided. They also avoided the term *synagoge*, to speak of the new Body of Christ, the Church. This is significant, in that the Septuagint, which had such a profound effect on the writers of the New Testament, uses the word *ekklesia* interchangeably with *synagoge*, to translate the Hebrew words for "assembly" or "congregation."[33] The original meaning of *ekklesia* was "the lawful assembly in a free Greek city of all those possessed of the rights of citizenship, for the transaction of public affairs."[34] The first usage of *ekklesia* in the New Testament is found in Matthew 16:18: "Upon this rock I will build my church." It is followed two chapters later in Jesus' teaching on church discipline, "tell it to the church" (18:17). In neither case is the church defined. The explanation of the Christian *ekklesia* comes in the book of Acts and the Epistles. Barr argues that the fact that *ekklesia* is one of the words used in the LXX to translate the Hebrew *qahal*[35] was likely because of "its general surface meaning of 'assembly' and corresponded simply to an understanding of *qahal* as 'assembly.'"[36] *qahal* itself did not have an inherently religious meaning, and was even used for the assemblies of the enemies of God (Psalm 26:5; 38:7).[37] Barr goes on to say that neither the usage of the Hebrew *qahal* nor its Greek translation *ekklesia* in the Bible denote anything about "the people of God" or "the Israel of God."[38]

The word, itself, however, was obviously understood by its Greek hearers, much in the same way that the word *baptizo* was understood to its Greek hearers. Radmacher explains, "The word *ekklesia* was not a creation of the Christian church. When the Christian church annexed it for its purposes, *ekklesia* was already a word with a history, and a double history – both Jewish and Greek."³⁹ Erickson says the same thing.⁴⁰ Part of this history was the Septuagint. Again, Radmacher explains, "Thus, when the writers of the New Testament, whose Bible was the Septuagint, used *ekklesia*, they were not inventing a new term. They found the term in common use and simply employed what was at hand.⁴¹ Even in its usage in the LXX, *ekklesia* does not have a religious connotation. It was called together, it appears, as deliberative entity. To be a part of the *ekklesia*, one had to be present at the assembly.⁴²

It remains, for the purposes of this writing, to note the concept lying behind the Greek world's understanding of the word *ekklesia*. Liddell and Scott define the *ekklesia* as "an assembly duly summoned."⁴³ Campbell states that "even in New Testament times the specific sense, of an assembly of the citizens, continued to be the most common meaning of the word."⁴⁴ The concept of democracy is frequently attached to the word in its secular usage,⁴⁵ but even if *ekklesia* did not always mean a democratic assembly, it was an assembly in which all persons called had a voice.⁴⁶ The *ekklesia*, whatever its makeup, was a decision-making body. In Athens, it even determined who its generals would be.⁴⁷ The churches throughout Greece, Rome, and western Asia Minor would have understood the word *ekklesia* as a popular assembly.⁴⁸ Campbell states, ". . . even in New Testament times the specific sense, of an assembly of the citizens, continued to be the most common meaning of the word."⁴⁹ By the time of the New Testament the republican era was over and emperors ruled, but the concept of the rule of the assembly was still widespread in the Latin language. Rome's armies had conquered the Mediterranean world under the standard, "Senate and People of Rome." In the Roman republic "Adult male citizens had the right to vote to elect the annual magistrates, to make laws, to declare war and peace and . . . to try citizens on serious charges."⁵⁰

An opposing view of this meaning of the word *ekklesia* is presented by Kevin Giles. He argues that instead of carrying any notions of an assembly, much less anything democratic, the word *ekklesia* signifies primarily the Christian community.⁵¹ The meaning of *ekklesia* itself is not so determinative for the concept of the church as is the combination of several ideas in the New Testament, including "the called-ones," "the body of Christ," "the people of God," and "the fellowship" among others.[52] Though Giles is talking about the whole concept of the Church, not just church government, his ideas necessarily enter into the discussion.

For Giles the New Testament meaning of *ekklesia* has little basis in its secular usage. He argues primarily from its usage in the Septuagint and secondarily from Qumran texts.[53] The Greek word *ekklesia*, he notes, is used in the LXX to translate the Hebrew *qahal*. But the Hebrew *qahal* itself modifies its meaning in later Old Testament books, to replace the word *edah*, and signify the covenant community, instead of meaning "the assembly."[54] Nehemiah 13:1 actually anticipates the New Testament title, "the Church of God."[55]

In the first place, Giles needs to offer more reasoning for giving the secular usage of *ekklesia* no place in the New Testament meaning.[56] Though he stresses the history of the word and cites the argument of James Barr on the subject,[57] he gives little basis for passing over the secular usage, whose history was going on at the same time.[58] He also winds up with a conclusion different from Barr's about the meaning of the *ekklesia*.[59] Secondly, as Giles argues from Old Testament passages, in several instances he overlooks statements in the beginning of the context of the passage in question, where the action of assembling is clearly signified.[60] Thirdly, thirty instances of the use of the word *qahal* in 1 Kings and 1 and 2 Chronicles, translated by the Greek *ekklesia* in the LXX, contradict Giles position (since the Chronicles were written later in the history of the Old Testament). These he disregards, as it were, with the wave of the hand, by the statement, "the scene painted is an ideal one."[61] The Chronicles however, present it as history. Even if, for argument's sake, it is an idealized scene, the usage is "assembly." Giles, who otherwise is quite thorough in his scholarship, needs a better argument in this last case.

Finally, Giles identifies *edah* as meaning "the covenant people of God."[62] But he fails to point out that the Hebrew *edah* frequently means "assembly" (e.g., Num. 10:2-3; 20:8; Judges

21:10; 1 Kings 12:20; Psalm 7:7). "It is used for groups and assemblies of nations, particularly where their power is in view."[63] It is also used for a group of evildoers (e.g., Num. 26:9; Psalm 22:17; Job 15:34).[64] It can mean a mob (Psalm 86:14) or a herd of cattle (Psalm 68:30). The general meaning of *edah* is "a congregation, properly a company assembled together by appointment, or acting concertedly."[65] On the other hand, *qahal* can denote more than an assembly. It can mean a company, assembled for religious purposes (e.g. Psalm 22:23) or a congregation, as an organized body.[66] This last meaning occurs as early as Exodus 12:6 and Leviticus 16:17. Lewis states, "*qahal* and *edah* seem to be synonymous for all practical purposes."[67] Therefore, even if Giles is correct that *qahal* later replaced *edah*, in the Hebrew Old Testament, it would in no way change the typical meaning of "assembly" for *qahal* and thus *ekklesia* in the New Testament. *Qahal* had at least three different meanings, but predominantly "assembly," and *edah* often had this meaning as well.

It still remains a significant matter that the LXX translators never used *ekklesia* to translate *edah*, but Giles has not, in the estimation of this author, helped us better understand why.[68] A far better answer is given by Radmacher, who bases his conclusions on the exhaustive studies of *ekklesia* in the LXX by Hort[69] and Baker.[70] He states,

> Thus, the only place the two words can be compared (i.e., the mutual translation by *synagoge*) the distinctive element of *qahal* seems to be the necessity of a physical meeting for a specific purpose, immediately or remotely displaying the prerogatives of autonomous action.[71]

With regard to the use of *ekklesia* itself in the LXX, Radmacher points out that on the basis of these two exhaustive studies, "All uses of the word never go beyond the simple meaning of *an assembly*."[72]

Giles is right in his book that far more enters into the concept of the church than the word, *ekklesia*. However, when he uses the LXX to come to his conclusion that believers in New Testament times understood *ekklesia* as "the covenant community" rather than "the assembly," he is making precisely the error Barr calls "reading the maximum possible theological content into a linguistic choice."[73]

One more matter needs to be considered pertaining to the idea of democratic thinking in New Testament times: the Jewish people themselves understood the concept of popular government.[74] Neither priestly nor kingly functions were democratic in ancient Israel. But by the time of the New Testament, the practice of electing seven Archons for each town's leadership, was probably long established in Judah and Galilee. These Archons were chosen by all the people of the town.[75] Baron states that the idea of popular approval or even popular choice of rulers stretches back to a time before the New Testament.

> Without directly adumbrating the modern doctrine of the sovereignty of the people, even ancient rabbinical theory recognized that, no matter how sanctified it was by the divine choice, the king's regime ultimately depended on its acceptance by the Jewish community at large. A Jewish king, in fact was not supposed to ascend the throne except by election of the Great Sanhedrin of seventy-one representing the whole people. These regulations pertaining to the monarchical regime were translated with necessary modifications, into the realm of communal legislation. . . . From Palestine westward the communal majority had its way, through elections or otherwise, of choosing, or even deposing, its communal leaders.[76]

The New Testament, while retaining the concept of "the assembly," as it used the word *ekklesia*, added to it modifiers: "of God," "in Christ" (1 Th. 1:1; 2:14; 2 Th. 1:1; 2:4).[77] These modifiers showed the Church's distinctness from the secular *ekklesia*. Radmacher concludes, "The Christian assembly may be defined, then, as a local assembly spiritually united in Christ, with an autonomous nature.[78]

One may rightly argue that no point has been established that the word *ekklesia* itself, in the New Testament, has to mean a popular assembly in a religious context. Its meaning is far broader and richer than that (e.g. Eph. 1:21-22: 5:25ff). Nevertheless, the connotations of a deliberative assembly attached to *ekklesia* are likewise very hard to brush away.

4. Examples of Self-Government from the New Testament.

1. The New Testament relates on different occasions how church officers were chosen by the whole assembly. One clear instance is the choice of the first deacons. "But select from among you (ἐπισκέψασθε), brethren, seven men . . . . And the statement found approval with the whole congregation (πάντος του πλήθους); and they chose (ἐξελέξαντο) Stephen . . . ." Bauer, Arndt, Gingrich and Danker's *Greek-English Lexicon* (hereafter designated BAGD) points out that *plethos*, in this instance, is a technical term in the New Testament, meaning the Christian congregation. All members were involved in the process.

John MacArthur, Jr. argues that the selection of the first deacons was not a congregational choice.[79] The authors of *A Biblical Theology of the Church* also argue against the idea that anything like a vote was taken in this instance. They do so in the following way:

> The key to all of this is the word "select (*episkeptomai*). The preposition *epi* means "over" and *skeptomai* comes from the word *skopos*, "scope." Put together, these words could be translated "to look over," or "to skeptically analyze." . . . Nowhere is the word *episkeptomai* in any form used in the sense of voting.[80]

The writers are correct in defining *episkeptomai* the way they do.[81] But one must understand the word can also very well mean "appoint to an office" or "choose." In the LXX it most certainly had that meaning (Nu. 4:27, 32: 16:5; 27:16; Neh. 7:1).[82] In Acts 15:14 James uses the word to describe God's action which led to his *selecting*. "God visited (*episkepsato*) to take (*labein*) out of the Gentiles a people for his name."

The writers are also wrong in making this word "the key" to understanding this passage. There are, in fact, several words that are key to understanding this passage, in addition to the sentence structure. Moreover, even if the proper translation of *episkeptomai* is "inspect," the Jerusalem congregation interpreted it as meaning also "to select." Without further instructions, they wound up, as a congregation, "choosing" (*exelexanto*) seven deacons. This last Greek word is the same as is used in Ephesians 1:4 to speak of God's electing of believers, in Luke 6:13 and John

6:70 of Jesus choosing the twelve, and in Deuteronomy 4:37 (LXX) of God's choosing of Israel.[83] In fact, in the New Testament *eklegomai* conveys only the idea of "choose." The apostles were more than satisfied with the action of the multitude, and proceeded to lay their hands on the chosen men (v.6).[84] *A Biblical Theology of the Church* agrees that the congregation made the selection of the seven deacons.[85] One wonders then why there is so much insistence made that there was no vote taken.

It can hardly be clearer, that the whole congregation made the decision. What method 5000 people used to come up with seven deacons is irrelevant to the truth presented. A body of people can designate a decision by hand, by ballot, by voice, or by consensus, or perhaps another method. They are all valid. Beyer concludes,

> The process described is of decisive significance in the history of Christian organization, since here for the first time we have an appointment, not through a call of the incarnate or risen Lord, nor through the self-attestation of the charismatic Spirit in a Christian, but by the election of the members of the congregation.[86]

Fung also emphasizes the significance of this event, calling it "a typical example of how the Church may be guided by the Holy Spirit in the formation of new institutions, in this case the creation of a new office with appropriate functions to which suitable persons were elected."[87]

A second instance of selecting officers by the church was the choice of two candidates to fill the office of Apostle vacated by Judas (Acts 1:15-23). All 120 of the assembled Christians, not just the apostles, participated in proposing[88] two men as candidates (v.23). Spencer notes,

> The appointment of a successor for Judas occurs not behind closed apostolic doors but 'among the believers' numbering about 120 (Acts 1:15). Peter, to be sure, takes the lead and stipulates the qualifications for enrollment in the Twelve, but ultimately 'they propose' (ἔστησαν) two candidates (1:23; cf. 6:6), 'they pray' (προσευξάμενοι) for divine guidance (1:24), and 'they cast' (ἔδωκαν) lots to determine the choice (1:26).[89]

This action was no simple human invention. Peter based it on his understanding of God's Word (Psalm 69:26; 109:8). He looked at the event as a fulfillment of God's Word (v.16): "It is therefore necessary" (v.21). Jesus had said while on earth that the twelve apostles would sit with him upon twelve thrones (Mt. 19:28). The twelve were anticipating the soon return of Jesus to set up his kingdom. To fulfill their work, they needed a twelfth apostle: "a witness with us of his resurrection."(1:22).

It is instructive to note what the group felt they had as capabilities, and where they saw their limits. The whole 120 Christians settled on two men: Joseph and Matthias (1:23) and "put them forth" *estesan*. BAGD defines this usage of *histemi* as, "put forward, propose for a certain purpose: the candidates for election to apostleship."[90] But the 120 did not feel capable of making the final choice of a twelfth apostle. This they petitioned the Lord to do himself, through the process of the lot. Thus the group did the nominating but not the final choosing (most people do not realize that the ancient democracy in Athens also chose most of its officers by lot).[91] Later in Acts 6, for the offices of deacon, the whole congregation in Jerusalem made the final decision. Kistenmaker notes that after the outpouring of the Holy Spirit on the day of Pentecost, the practice of using the lot ceased.[92] The subsequent baptism in the Holy Spirit may be significant for the fact that the church later made a full choice of its officers.

Some Bible teachers view Peter's teaching and the action of the 120 as an error, and propose that Paul was to have been the twelfth apostle.[93] In addition to the above-mentioned rationale for the action, it must be pointed out that Paul, though an apostle, did not consider himself one of the twelve (1 Cor. 15:8; Gal. 1:15-24). Instead, he viewed himself as the apostle to the Gentiles (Gal. 2:9). Luke, the close companion of Paul, used the term "the twelve" for the original eleven plus Matthias (Acts 2:14; 6:2). Kistenmacker notes, "The difference between Paul and the Twelve is obvious: Paul submits his work to the scrutiny of the apostles (see Gal. 1:18; 2:1-2, 7-10)."[94] The concept of Paul as the twelfth apostle has some logic to it, but it is difficult to defend from the New Testament.

Though the matter of selection of elders will be taken up later, here it is helpful to consider what Clement of Rome said about the way elders were chosen in the New Testament times. The words of Clement are not normative for the Church, but they are significant in that they were written before the end of the first century.[95] Since some elders were still living from the time of Paul, Clement could not have deceived his readers on this point. He tells the Corinthian church,

> Our apostles likewise knew, through our Lord Jesus Christ, that there would be strife over the bishop's office. For this reason, therefore, having received complete foreknowledge, they appointed the officials mentioned earlier and afterwards they gave the offices a permanent character; that is, if they should die, other approved men should succeed to their ministry. Those, therefore, who were appointed by them or, later on, by other reputable men *with the consent of the whole church* .... (italics added).[96]

2. The entire local assembly determines what teaching they will accept as true. Of course, a church in the New Testament sense accepts the entire Old and New Testaments as true. But in this case, the discussion is about the interpretation of the Old and New Testaments. The whole church in Jerusalem participated in the proceedings during the controversy over the place of the Law of Moses in the lives of Christians. Paul and Barnabas came to the meeting as representatives of the Antioch church (and well they needed to be there, as the validity of their entire ministry was put in question by the controversy). "And when they arrived at Jerusalem, they were received by the church and the apostles and the elders, and they reported all that God had done with them" (Acts 15:4). The meeting in Acts 15 was not a council of churches. Rather it was a gathering of the Jerusalem church, with representatives from the Antioch church in attendance. All the other churches, however, took its decision as binding.

All the members of the Jerusalem church together made the determination about their theological direction pertaining to the applications of the Law of Moses for Christians: "Then it seemed good to the apostles and the elders, with the whole church, to choose men from among them to send to Antioch with Paul and

Barnabas . . . and they sent this letter by them" (pastoral leadership legitimately exercised, 15:22-23). In fact, the Apostles and the Elders at Jerusalem formulated the statement (15:23), but the whole church participated in the discussion, the end decision, and in the affirmation of the letter's contents.[97] The Jerusalem church was composed of people who had experienced the baptism of the Holy Spirit (Acts 2:1-4,38, cf. 11:15-17), and had submitted themselves to the teaching of the Apostles as a rule of life (2:41-42). They were fully capable of interpreting Scripture for themselves, particularly in matters pertaining to salvation (Acts 15:1; 1 Jn. 2:26-27; 4:6). That the Apostles brought the Church into this doctrinal discussion was crucial for the future of the church. Not to have done so would have been a tacit denial of their ability to interpret Scripture, and to relegate this activity to Apostles and Elders.[98]

3. In New Testament times, missionaries and representatives were sent out by the entire church (Acts 11:22; 13:1-3). It is significant to note that in the commissioning of Paul and Barnabas, the Twelve made no contribution (if the Episcopal view is correct, then the appointment of the Twelve would be expected). If it be argued that Barnabas was the representative of the Apostles in Antioch, it must likewise be noted that his representative function was irrelevant in this instance: he did not appoint or lay hands on anybody. Rather, Barnabas was appointed.[99] Longenecker's extended comment on this passage is a thorough argument on this point:

> Luke's literary style in these verses is somewhat clipped, and we could wish that he had given us more details. Luke does not tell us how the Spirit made his will known, though we may assume that it was through a revelation given to one of the believers. Neither does he tell us the nature of the special ministry the two were set apart for, though from what follows it is obvious that we are meant to understand that it was to be a mission to the Gentiles. Nor do we have the antecedent of the third person verbal suffix "they" (*apelysan*), and so we do not have the precise identification of the sentence's subject. Still, we may infer from the parallel usage in 15:2 (*etaxan*, "they appointed," where the antecedent is relatively clear from the context), and from the descriptions of early church government in 6:2-6 and

15:4-30 that the whole congregation, together with its leaders, was involved in attesting the validity of the revelation received, laid hands on the missioners, and sent them out. This is confirmed by the reference to the whole church in 14:27. For just as it was the whole church that sent them out, so it was the whole church the missioners reported to on returning to Antioch."[100]

Likewise, other representatives of churches were commissioned by the action of the whole church. This is implicit in the return sending of Paul and Barnabas: "And after they had spent time there, they were sent away from the brethren in peace to those who had sent them" (Acts 15:33) It is explicit in 1 Corinthians 16:3 and especially in 2 Corinthians 8:18-19:

> And we have sent along with him (Titus) the brother whose fame in the things of the gospel has spread through all the churches; and not only this, but he has also been appointed by the churches to travel with us in this in this gracious work, which is being administered by us for the glory of the Lord himself.

The passage just quoted has reference to Paul's collection for the Christians in Jerusalem. It is important to note that Paul makes the churches (not their officers) responsible for the appointment of this man to his representative work.[101] The word translated "appoint" is *cheirotoneo*, and means 1) elect or 2) appoint.[102] As this word only occurs two times in the New Testament (and never in the LXX), it is worthwhile to look to other sources to help define the meaning. Lohse points out that *cheirotoneo* is used by Isocrates, Demosthenes and Plato to signify a vote. It is likewise used in Josephus and by Philo (*De Praemiis et Poenis*, 54) simply to mean "appoint."[103] In the early second century Ignatius used the term to refer to officers selected by the whole congregation.[104] Of particular interest is the usage of *cheirotoneo* by Philo in *De Speciablibus Legibus, I*. In this passage, Philo relates a practice of Diaspora Jews which parallels the Christian practice instituted by Paul among the churches in Macedonia and Achaia.[105] In this instance, Philo had the election of representatives in view. As the context must determine the meaning of a word, this instance in 2 Corinthians 8:19 most likely refers to an election by churches, since several bodies chose one man. Furthermore, the parallel usage in Philo sheds light on how this practice might have taken place.

4. The whole Church is responsible to preserve spiritual truth: "I felt the necessity to write to you appealing that you contend earnestly for the faith . . ." (Jude 3). All Christians are to "test the spirits" (1 Jn. 4:1), that is, the spiritual source behind questionable teaching.[106] Paul praises the whole church in Corinth because they "hold firmly to the traditions, just as I delivered them to you" (1 Cor. 11:2). That which was committed to them included the ordinances (11:23). In Paul's view, the whole local assembly is "the pillar and ground of the truth" (1 Tim. 3:15). An overseer or elder, or group of the same is never viewed in this way in the New Testament. Ministers of the Gospel are *oikonomoi* ("stewards," 1 Tim. 1:7), but the local church is God's *oikos* "house." As James Denney notes, the church

> . . . is not united by offices, nor even by officials; it is not united by a documentary constitution or creed; it is not united by a uniform and all-embracing government – not one of these things is mentioned by the apostles. Christ's gifts to it for the maintenance and furtherance of its unity are not offices nor officials, but spiritually endowed men; it is not in the fellowship of a priestly or episcopal order – much less in the fellowship of a Pope – that it is one; it is one in the fellowship of the Holy Ghost.[107]

Unfortunately, this confession of Paul regarding the local church was superceded in time by a legal explanation invented by some of the Church Fathers, including Iranaeus[108] and Tertullian.[109] In their contentions with false teaching, they presented part of the basis of the true faith to be a documented succession of bishops for the churches from the time of the apostles. This was fixed once and for all in the Episcopal system by Cyprian: "The Church is in the Bishop and the Bishop in the Church." The Roman Church extended this concept one step further, making the Bishop of Rome the foundation for all church unity

> The Pope, Bishop of Rome and Peter's successor, is the perpetual and visible source and foundation of the unity both of the bishops and of the whole company of the faithful. For the

Roman Pontiff, by reason of his office as Vicar of Christ, and as pastor of the entire Church has full, supreme, and universal power over the whole Church, a power which he can always exercise unhindered.[110]

For this statement in the *Catechism,* any Scriptural reference is conspicuously absent. It is also in direct contrast to 1 Timothy 3:15. In response, the following argument of the Roman Catholic Hans Küng is significant:

All the faithful belong to the people of God; there must be no clericalization of the Church... If the Church is the true people of God, it is impossible to differentiate between "Church" and "laity," as though the laity were not in a very real sense "*laos*". .. It is striking that the word *laos* with the meaning "people of God" is so often used for the Christian community, whereas the word *laikos*, "layman"... simply does not occur in the New Testament.[111]

As an added thought, Alexander Hay points out that if Jesus had meant that Peter was to be the pontiff of the church, he would not have answered Peter's question about John's task with the response, "What is that to you?" (John 21:22).[112] The local church, the temple of God, indwelt by the Spirit of God (1 Cor. 3:16-17), is responsible together with all its members for maintaining its theological direction.

5. Finally, church discipline falls under the jurisdiction of the whole church (Mat. 18:15-17; cf. 1 Cor. 5:1-13). Paul states that it is the distinct responsibility of the members of the local church to conduct discipline: "Do you not judge those who are within? But those who are outside, God judges. Remove the wicked man from among yourselves" (1 Cor. 5:11-12). In the three steps of church discipline appointed by Christ in the book of Matthew, one individual takes initiative, is afterward helped by one or two more Christians, and lastly involves the whole church. One cannot find in this passage any reference to a step exclusively involving the elders, or any type of leadership council.[113] In 2 Corinthians 2:6, Paul says that the discipline on the erring member was brought to pass by "the majority."[114]

Lightfoot,[115] followed by Hughes,[116] point out that that 2 Corinthians 2:6 in and of itself has much to demonstrate about the government of the early church. Though Paul was not present government of the early church. Though Paul was not present for the discipline of a member of the church (1 Cor. 5), nevertheless he directed the proceedings, in which he instructed the church, they voted, and he announced the verdict, as it were. O'Brien likewise states, "The apostle gives his advice in no uncertain terms .... But the congregation itself is to make the decision."[117] Though one may argue with the scheme Lightfoot presents, it is nevertheless plain that one man was disciplined through a decision of the majority of the members of the Corinthian church.[118] If members of the church are capable of making decisions in matters so serious as church discipline, they must also be capable of making decisions together about other far less serious concerns, such as buildings, ministries, etc. Commenting on the Matthew passage, Hendricksen states,

> To be sure, the church "authorities" must take the lead. ... But when the proper time arrives, should they not in turn ask the congregation as a whole to be remembered in prayer, along with all the individuals concerned ... Without in any way shirking their own responsibilities or laying aside their own authority, should not the overseers recognize the *entire* body of believers (here locally organized) in all important matters? Is not this the clear meaning of, "Tell the church?"[119]

It is important to understand that Christ and the apostles laid down a method of discipline different from the Synagogue. One must acknowledge the fact that the early Christian believers brought much with them from their experience of synagogue life and order. However, the influence of the synagogue was also limited. The Church was not the synagogue, but a new entity. Vermes, Millar and Black point out,

> There is in any case no trace in Jewish congregations of anything resembling the way in which the full assembly of the Christian church at Corinth (1 Cor. 5), or the Qumran community (1QS 8:25-9:2), itself discussed and decided on individual cases of discipline and administration. Instead, this was done by the appropriate bodies, i.e. the elders of the congregation.[120]

The significance of this difference between the synagogue and the church and an explanation for the difference in operation will be taken up later.

Effects of the Self-Government of the Church

1. It tends to an increased awareness of the responsibility of personal evangelism.[121] Evangelism is an outworking of the activity of the Holy Spirit in the heart of the believer, in obedience to Christ's command to preach the Gospel to every creature. Teaching about this responsibility helps the believer to realize his responsibility. The example of believers who evangelize motivates others to do so as well. The same holds true for the conducive environment of the church in which the believer worships. It is significant to note the next action mentioned in the Book of Acts after the congregational choice of the first deacons: "And the word of God kept on spreading; and the number of the disciples continued to increase greatly in Jerusalem . . ." (6:7). It may be argued that this is simply an historical note by Luke. However, the following action mentioned about the whole church after Acts 6 is likewise significant: "Therefore, those who had been scattered went about preaching the word" (8:4). The early Church was filled with Christians who believed that they had a responsibility to one-another, to the church as a whole, and to the world as evangelists.

The official *Catechism* of the Catholic Church takes the opposite view of the role of the average church member in evangelism. In the section on "Hierarchical Constitution of the Church," it argues that only Christ can mandate to a person to preach the Gospel (the reference here is to Romans 10:14-15). It goes on to say, "This fact presupposes ministers of grace, authorized and empowered by Christ, from him bishops and priests receive the mission and faculty ("the sacred power") to act *in persona Christi capitis* . . ."[122]

Historical research well demonstrates that from AD 30 to AD 313 the Roman Empire was evangelized primarily by average Christians who shared their faith, not professional clergy.[123] Kennedy points out that the development of the hierarchy in the church following the first three centuries of the Church helped eliminate personal evangelism:

This is how the Church of Jesus Christ in 300 years accomplished the most amazing results. The whole pagan Roman Empire was undercut and overthrown by the power of the gospel of Christ which, on the lips of Christ-conquered disciples, crossed seas and deserts, pierced the darkest jungles, seeped into every city and town, and finally into the senate and the very palace of Rome itself – until a Christian Caesar was placed upon the throne. How? Because everyone was evangelizing. . . . .

By A.D. 300 the church had shown such tremendous strength and virility, and was spreading so swiftly, that it appeared the entire civilized world could be evangelized by A.D. 500. But something happened. Emperor Constantine in the year 313 issued the Edict of Toleration by which the long agonizing persecution of the Christians was at last brought to a halt. In the following decades numerous other edicts favoring the Christians were passed, until at last the whole Roman Empire was declared by fiat to be Christian. Thus millions of barbarians flooded into the church, bringing with them all of the pagan superstitions and heresies. They didn't even know the gospel. They had never experienced its transforming power and, of course, they could not go out and tell others about it. So, little by little, the idea arose that there was a division between the clergy and the laity, and that this task of evangelism was the job of the professionally trained individuals.[124]

This is presented to make the concept clear, that though many denominations with a hierarchical structure do evangelize, hierarchy by its very nature tends to eliminate the understanding that each Christian has the responsibility of evangelism.

2. Freedom of Conscience is given a broader opening. According to the argument of Hebrews chapter 9, because of the relationship of the New Testament believer to Jesus Christ as his High Priest, and because of the Lord's sacrifice, the believer's conscience is freed. He knows he is forgiven, and stands in a right relationship to God (9:9-14). He is free, on his own, to obey the commands of Scripture as he discovers them in the Bible. This doesn't eliminate the necessity of teachers. But it does give the believer more ability to act on his own. When, however, a person in the church takes over some part of the role of Christ as

mediator, the consciences of the believers will be to that extent bound.[125]

Cyprian, though a courageous Christian, was also one of the most important Church Fathers in developing the Episcopate. Lightfoot states that ". . . he raised it to a position of absolute independence, from which it has never since been deposed."[126] Cyprian claimed, " . . . the bishop is in the Church, and the Church in the bishop; and if any one be not with the bishop, . . . he is not in the Church."[127] Cyprian also claimed direct inspiration from the Lord,[128] and to be endowed with apostolic powers.[129] "Once elected his (the bishop's) authority was practically unchallengeable."[130] Everyone who opposed the bishop opposed the Lord. Thus the members of the church became doctrinally subject to the viewpoint of the clergy. Though Gibbon unfairly criticized Christians and uncritically praised pagan Roman religion, his acute observation on Cyprian's doctrine remains true:

> . . . the acquisition of such absolute command over the consciences and understanding of a congregation, however obscure or despised by the world, is more truly grateful to the pride of the human heart than the possession of the most despotic power imposed by arms and conquest on a reluctant people.[131]

One hundred years after Cyprian the author(s) of the *Apostolic Constitutions* wrote to bishops, "You are to the laity prophets, rulers, governors, and kings; the mediators between God and His faithful people."[132] This sort of teaching was widely accepted in Christendom at that time.

The extreme form of the exercise of this authority can be historically observed centuries later in the Inquisition. The same belief or attitude is present in the leadership of modern-day cults. Unfortunately it is also present among some pastors or elders of independent congregations in our day. When in a church controversy they may argue, "The Lord has spoken to me, so do as I say." Protestants, particularly independents, have historically opposed the idea of a pope. With this in mind, Ray Stedman notes, "If a pope over the whole church is bad, a pope in every church is no better."[133] Kenneth Gangel states the positive side of the truth: "An objective-oriented ministry steers away from autocratic dominance because it knows that God speaks through people, not just pastors."[134] Church leaders need to listen to their members. When they shut out the viewpoint of the people in the church, they begin to take their church on the first steps of a hierarchy like that of Cyprian. Before church leaders initiate a new program or practice in their church, they need to wait until the whole church is ready. The Spirit of God dwells in every Christian. He is fully able to lead them.

3. Still another advantage of the self-governing church is that every member takes part in worship and service (Rom. 12:5-6; 1 Cor. 14:26). There are principles about corporate worship of the Church in the New Testament. It is to be done "decently and in order" (1 Cor. 14:40). Public prayer, public reading of the Bible, exhortation and teaching are essential in the service, according to Paul (1 Tim. 2:1; 4:13).[135] But there are few details about required form. Members are to be given the opportunities to share about their walk with the Lord or their learning from Scripture (1 Cor. 14:26 – obviously Paul did not mean that everyone should say something every Sunday morning).[136] According to the New Testament, every member of a church should be doing service in that church. When each member has a voice in church affairs, and can decide together with the group about church actions, he will be much more likely to take on ministry as his responsibility. If, instead, all ideas come from the leaders, the members begin to feel like slaves: not slaves of Christ, but of the church leadership.

Why Do Some Find the Self-Government of the Local Church a False Principle?

First, throughout Church history many other forms of church government were developed. As has already been noted, the further the development of the church through history, until the time of the Reformation, the stronger and more detailed hierarchy became. The episcopacy had already become entrenched by AD 250, and is therefore over 1750 years old. Morris points out that "More Christians accept episcopacy than any other form of church government."[137] It would therefore be most commonly thought of as the right form of church government. The Presbyterian structure had its development beginning with the Reformation, thus being 500 years old.

Christian publications have rarely given notice that there have been many independent, self-governing churches throughout the centuries (usually suppressed and persecuted). Typical of this misunderstanding is the statement by Morris: "Congregationalism as a system appeared after the Reformation."[138] Morris no doubt was thinking of the development of Congregationalism among the English Puritans at the outset of the 17th Century. But the Anabaptist churches, which began with the Reformation, were congregational. Estep notes, "The idea finds expression in both the writings of Huebmaier and Grebel by 1524."[139] Mennonite churches, which have come directly out of the Anabaptist movement, continue to practice congregational government. The seed thoughts of Congregationalism are found in the teachings of Martin Luther. Indeed, he was the original Congregationalist of the Reformation.[140] Even Strauch, who emphasizes a return to the New Testament pattern of church leadership, mentions Calvin's teachings, then George Mueller's efforts at reestablishing biblical eldership. He fully overlooks the Anabaptists.[141] Nevertheless, for Christians today it is more important to follow the Bible than to follow tradition, as Eduard Schweizer poignantly states:

> Church history will help in the task of interpretation, but it is not a second source of revelation. It is an interpretation, which is to be heard with the greatest respect, but which cannot absolve us from constantly returning to the source; for the history of the Church can just as easily be the history of a constantly renewed understanding as of a constantly repeated misunderstanding.[142]

The New Testament clearly shows that there were decision-making processes in the church which involved the entire local body.

Second, some have the view that the self-government concept, with a pastor leading the church, gives the pastor too much power. He will easily misuse his authority and become a dictator. The authors of *A Biblical Theology of the Church* single out Baptists in particular for the error of "one pastor" in the church, and give this as "one of the key reasons (for) dysfunction in the local assembly."[143] Indeed, some pastors who have been elected by a congregation later behave themselves in a dictatorial way. But McLachlan makes a correct comparison:

> There is no doubt that a dictatorial oligarchy (rule by a few), which operates on the basis of congregational immunity, is more dangerous than a dictatorial autocracy (rule by one), where significant proposals are subject to congregational democracy.[144]

In fact, the criticism cuts both ways. Quite often pastors who have desired a biblical direction in their church have been hamstrung in their efforts by a board of elders that was worldly and resisted the leading of the Lord.

Third, some argue that the self-government of the local church leads quickly to divisiveness. The continual open discussions and argumentative atmosphere involved arouse factionalism and dissatisfaction.[145] Interestingly, this criticism is the identical one which despots used for centuries against democratic forms of political government, as pointed out by Alexander Hamilton in the *Federalist Papers*.[146] In answer to this criticism, it would be helpful to consider the church in Corinth. This church was founded by Paul. Shortly after he left, strife and divisions (1 Cor. 1:10; 10:11; *schismata*) took place. Either Paul taught the Church in Corinth the processes of self-government, or he taught them another type of church government, which just as quickly led to divisiveness. In fact, every form of church government has experienced major divisions throughout history to the present hour. But the danger of divisions doesn't depend upon the nature of church government. Rather, it depends upon people who are fleshly or worldly-minded. That is precisely what Paul (1 Cor. 3) and James (Ja. 4) teach us.

Fourth, some argue that the self-government of the local church carries with it a political character because of candidates, votes, and so forth. They present examples from the Bible in which the majority opposed the will of God (e.g. Numbers 13-14).[147] But these are simply methods of group decision-making. And every type of church government (no exceptions) can be identified as political. There are many examples of one person, or a small number of persons, leading the whole group astray. Take for example various instances when the kings of Israel and Judah led their people into idolatry. Rehoboam's determination to show everyone who was boss, instead of accepting the proposals of his people, is a clear example of foolishness (1 Ki. 12). In 1 Samuel 8 the Elders of Israel forced Samuel to set up a king in Israel, something which displeased God. The Elders of Samaria agreed with Jezebel to prosecute and murder an innocent man (1 Ki. 21:8-13). The "one man show" of Jehoiada, the high priest, brought about the end of baalamic tyranny in Judah. After his death, the rulers of Israel (which may be interpreted as "elders")[148] quickly turned the heart of the king to idolatry (2 Chr. 23-24). The evil things that individuals or groups do in no way confirm or condemn a particular system. Rather, the prevalence of wicked behavior in a system of government makes it suspect.

Fifth, some argue that the self-government of the local church demands a spirituality not possessed by the average church member. Note the following statement: "This type of organization must assume that all its members are actually filled with the Holy Spirit, on whom they faithfully depend for guidance. This has led to a liberal approach in the outworking of the Congregational system."[149] While this statement implies that most church members are not sufficiently filled with the Holy Spirit, it also begs the question that all elders are indeed filled with the Holy Spirit (for in the next paragraph the author argues that a plurality of elders is the key to restoring a church to the New Testament order). It likewise overlooks the fact that essentially every kind of church structure has experienced its fall into false teaching or apostasy. The New Testament doctrine, that every believer is indwelt by the Holy Spirit and anointed by the Holy Spirit for the understanding of spiritual truth,[150] is a key to understanding why the apostles so highly trusted the decision-making abilities of the people in the congregation. It is fascinating to observe this phenomenon in the book of Acts. Ridderbos states,

> That the church does not have to submit itself as an underage or dependent multitude under the authorities set over it, but has the power and calling to upbuild itself, is fundamental for a

correct insight into the Pauline concept of the church and of the order and law that are to obtain in its midst.[151]

One might extend this to the whole of the New Testament corpus, not just Pauline theology.

There is a corollary to this last objection against the self-government of the church. Since democracy in the church allows the membership a hand in determining the spiritual direction of the church, the audience is sovereign and doctrinal error is the inevitable result. David Wells expresses this idea in his book, *No Place for Truth*. Building upon the analysis of Nathan Hatch,[152] he says that after the American Revolution,

> The Baptists, Methodists, and Disciples of Christ were out on the highways and byways winning the soul of America. They profoundly affected the nation. There was, however, a cost to be paid in the upheavals that accompanied these ministries. This ambitious drive produced some savage anti-clericalism, for example . . . By 1855 . . . the Methodists and Baptists together constituted 70 percent of the Protestant population – a predominance that has largely persisted to the present day. . . . What this meant – and what it continues to mean – is that at the psychological center of much evangelical faith are two ideas that are also at the heart of the practice of democracy: (1) the audience is sovereign, and (2) ideas find legitimacy and value only within the marketplace. Ideas have no intrinsic or self-evident value; it is the people's *right* to give ideas their legitimacy.[153]

Wells' book has sounded a much-needed alarm for American Christians. But his broad-sweeping indictment of Baptist, Methodist and Disciples of Christ theology is a caricature rather than an analysis. Why is it that Presbyterians, Anglicans and Lutherans have likewise suffered major departures from the truth in their American ranks, if Baptist and Methodist theology and evangelism is so much to blame for relativism in belief? Why is it that on the European continent, where Baptists and Methodists have such little representation, departures from faith in the Bible preceded those in America by nearly a century, and have been far more thorough? Why is Europe the only place in the world where Christianity is receding in numbers? Perhaps the audience is sovereign in the Baptist, Methodist and Disciples of Christ churches that have departed from the faith, but none of these churches operated according to this concept in their founding.

There is, to be sure, a sovereignty of the membership among the Baptists, the Disciples of Christ and some of the Methodists (one may also include the Mennonites, the Assemblies of God, the Evangelical Free Church, etc.), just as there was a sovereignty of the citizens in Athens. But this is not the same as the sovereignty of the audience. In the Athenian democracy the citizens, even as a group, were under the law, as historian Robert Browning points out:

> We must bear in mind that though the Assembly exercised sovereign power, it did so within a framework of law. It could not pass a resolution without a previous draft prepared by the Council. It could not pass resolutions which were in conflict with the laws which it had already approved.[154]

Moreover, for the Baptists, Disciples of Christ and other congregational churches, the sovereignty of the congregation was always a sovereignty under the rule of the Christ of the Bible. That their preachers went to the masses with the Gospel was out of sincere obedience to Christ's command and in imitation of his example. They were following in the footsteps of the great open air preacher, George Whitefield. Equating their evangelistic methodology, or ecclesiology, with market place motivation in Christianity is an anachronism, and not based on a serious encounter with the writings of their theologians.[155]

Wells also neglects something pointed out by Hatch, that the preachers of the Baptist, Methodist and Disciples of Christ movements as well as others changed the audience. They helped develop a Bible-reading public in Americans as they moved west. They also brought theology to the level of the average person.[156]

In 1848 Alexis de Tocqueville wrote that on Sundays nearly everyone in the United States stopped his work, went to church, and then afterward went home and read his Bible.[157] The Baptists, Methodists and Disciples of Christ had as much to do with this state of affairs as any other group of churches. Arnold Toynbee went so far as to say, "The modern English-speaking world was saved in the eighteenth and nineteenth centuries by the Methodists."[158]

There are many forms of church government which find no place in the New Testament pattern: hierarchy, the episcopate, a pastor who is a dictator, or an authoritarian board of elders which only answers to itself. The Bible teaches a different kind of church government and leadership, that is, congregational. It is clear from the New Testament that many types of decisions were made by the entire local assembly together. It is also clear that churches throughout the Roman empire functioned with decentralized decision-making processes during the time of the apostles. Through the centuries many churches have had the courage to adopt this type of church government.

Recommended for Further Study

Radmacher, Earl. *The Nature of the Church.* Hayesville, NC: Schoettle, 1996. (Excellent general volume on ecclesiology. It is thorough, scholarly and readable: understandable to the theologian and non-theologian alike. It was for years the textbook on the subject at Dallas Seminary.)

Lightfoot, James B. *St. Paul's Epistle to the Philippians.* Grand Rapids: Zondervan, 1953 rprn. (In particular, his essay "The Christian Ministry.")

Cowen, Gerald P. *Who Rules The Church? Examining Congregational Leadership and Church Government.* Nashville: Broadman and Holman, 2003. (Cowen is a Southern Baptist theologian. His book presents the position of congregational government, concentrating most of its discussion on the role of pastor/elder. Two very good appendices, written by fellow professors trace congregational practice from 1963 back to the beginning of the Reformation).

Saucy, Robert. *The Church in God's Program.* Chicago: Moody, 1972. (A very good all-around small volume on ecclesiology: worthwhile for pastor, student, and studious church member)

O'Brien, P.T. "Church," *Dictionary of Paul and His Letters.* Gerald Hawthorne and Ralph Martin, eds. Downers Grove: InterVarsity, 1993: 123-131. (Well-done scholarly presentation of the subject in brief)

Kuen, Alfred. *I Will Build My Church.* Chicago: Moody, 1971. (Both exegetical and historical, by a European Free Church scholar.)

Basden, Paul and David S. Dockery, Eds. *The People of God: Essays on the Believer's Church.* Nashville: Broadman, 1991. (This volume, now out of print, is written by Baptist scholars and deals with a number of Free Church issues. It includes historical studies on various themes of ecclesiology. There are a variety of perspectives among the different writers.).

Nuttall, Clayton L. *The Weeping Church* Schaumberg: Regular Baptist Press, 1985. (This book was written out of a concern about attacks on Congregationalism as well as familiarity with numerous church conflicts. It is an emphatic presentation of the Congregationalist position. Nuttall explains Congregationalism as "Body-life". He emphasizes respect for the pastor. Exactly how congregational decision-making is supposed to take place is not well defined. It is, nevertheless, one of the few recent works on the whole subject)

Spencer, F. Scott. *The Portrait of Philip in Acts,* JSONT. Sheffield: University of Sheffield, 1992. (This is a technical study dealing in depth with polity as found in the book of Acts).

Decker, Rodney J. "Polity and the Elder Issue," *Grace Theological Journal*, 9.2 (Fall, 1988): 257-277.

Morris, Leon. "Church Government," *Evangelical Dictionary of Theology*. Walter Elwell, ed. Grand Rapids: Baker, 1984: 238-241.

Lynch, John E. "Church, Church Polity," *The Encyclopedia of Religion*, Vol. 3. Mircea Eliade, Ed. New York: Macmillan, 1987: 473-485 (Explains the polity of major protestant denominations.)

Schmidt, K.L. "ἐκκλησία," *Theological Dictionary of the New Testament,* III, Geoffrey Bromiley, trans. Grand Rapids: Eerdmans, 1965: 501-536.

Notes

[1] Ulrich Schwarz, "Wir sind das Volk," *Spiegiel Special* II/1990, 13. "Der Eingang der Nikolaikirche mitten in der Leipizger Innenstadt bietet ein farbenpraechtiges Bild: Vor dem Portal liegen in dichten Buendeln Herbstblumen in leuchtenden Farben, dazwischen brennen Kerzen. Dazwischen hat einer mit sauberer Handschrift einen Bibelvers geheftet: 'Zur Freiheit hat uns Christus befreit, Bleibt daher fest und lasst euch nicht von neuem das Joch der Knechtschaft auflegen.' Verbluehen fuer jene jungen Leipziger, die in den letzten Wochen verhaftet wurden, weil sie sich in Demokratie geuebt hatten."

² Like all views of church order, the congregational position suffers from the spread of a fair amount of false information. Typical is the following statement by Larry Taylor: "The congregational form of church government is an American invention and appeals to our American sense of democracy." Larry Taylor, "What Calvary Teaches: Church Government." (internet document) http://www.calvarychapel.com/cheyenne/Books/WCTGover.html.

³ William R. Estep, *The Anabaptist Story* (Grand Rapids: Eerdmans, 1975), 190.

⁴ The Cambridge Platform, the earliest statement of the Congregational position on American soil, states that the power of the Church "is in the hands of the brethren, formally and immediately from Christ." V.2., quoted by Henry Dexter, *Congregationalism* (Boston: Congregational Publishing Society, 1865), 40.

⁵ See, for instance, Peter Carroll, *Religion and the Coming American Revolution* (Toronto: Ginn-Blaisdell, 1970); Sanford H. Cobb, *The Rise of Religious Liberty in America* (New York: Cooper Square, 1968, rprn. from 1902); William W. Sweet, *Religion in the Development of American Culture*, (New York: Charles Scribner's Sons, 1952); Alan Heimert, *Religion and the American Mind* (Cambridge, MA: Harvard University, 1966); William G. McLoughlin, *New England Dissent: 1630-1833*, Vol. I&II, (Cambridge, MA: Harvard University, 1971); Charles M. Snow, *Religious Liberty in America* (Washington, DC: Review and Herald, 1914).

⁶ Ignaz Doellinger, *Beitraege zur Sektengeschichte des Mittelalters*, vol. I (Darmstadt: Wissenschaftliche Buchgesellschaft, 1968, rprn. from 1890 ed.), 75-110. Robert Ian Moore, "Petrus von Bruis," *Theologische Realenzyklopaedie*, Vol. 26 (Berlin: de Gruyter, 1996), 286. David Schaff, *History of the Christian Church*, Vol. 5 (New York: Scribner's, 1907), 96-102; 481-486. "Arnold of Brescia," *Oxford Dictionary of the Christian Church*, 2nd ed. F.L. Cross and E.A. Livingstone, eds. (Oxford: Oxford University, 1982), 92.

⁷ Philip Schaff, *A History of the Christian Church*, Vol. IV (Grand Rapids: Eerdmans, 1974 rprn.), 72-77. "The volume, which was written in two months, was as audacious as any of the earlier writings of Luther. For originality and boldness of statement the Middle Ages has nothing superior to offer." 73.

⁸ F.F. Bruce, *The English Bible* (New York: Oxford University, 1970), 12-13.

⁹ Ibid., 13.

¹⁰ Schaff, 320-321.

¹¹ Herold J. Grimm, *The Reformation Era: 1500-1650* (New York: Macmillan, 1973), 140-141. Luther's teaching that each church should choose its own pastor is found in his tract, "Das eine christliche Versammlung oder Gemeinde Recht und Macht habe, alle Lehre zu beurteilen und Lehrer zu berufen, ein-und abzuzetzen: Grund und Ursache aus der Schrift," *Martin Luthers Ausgewählte Werke*, Vol. 3 (Munich: Christian Raiser Verlag, 1938), 220-229.

¹² David Cornick, "The Reformed Elder," *The Expository Times* 98.8 (1987), 236.

¹³ This is stated in the London Baptist Confession, 1596. See Steven Prescott, "Ecclesiology among the Baptists in Great Britain and America," in Gerald P. Cowen, *Who Rules the Church?* Nashville: Broadman and Holman, 2003), 134.

¹⁴ Nathan O. Hatch, *The Democratization of American Christianity* (New Haven: Yale, 1989), 102-113.

¹⁵ Ibid., 113.

[16] "A Declaration of the Faith and Order Owned and Practiced in the Congregational Churches in England," Philip Schaff, ed. *The Creeds of Christendom*, Vol. III (Grand Rapids: Baker, 1990 rprn.), 724.

[17] Clinton E. Arnold, *The Colossian Syncretism* (Grand Rapids: Baker Books, 1996), 259.

[18] Ibid., 260.

[19] Leon Morris, "Church Government," *Evangelical Dictionary of Theology*, Walter Elwell, ed. (Grand Rapids: Baker, 1984), 240.

[20] Earl Radmacher, *The Nature of the Church* (Hayesville, NC: Schoettle, 1996), 346.

[21] "Symposium: The Body Christ Heads," *Christianity Today*, 1 (August 15, 1957), 9.

[22] Robert Saucy, *The Church in God's Program* (Chicago: Moody, 1972), 116.

[23] Kevin Giles, *What on Earth is the Church?* (Downers Grove: InterVarsity, 1995), 14.

[24] Ibid.

[25] Eduard Schweizer, *Church Order in The New Testament*, Frank Clarke, Transl. (London: SCM Press, 1961), 176.

[26] Dexter, 39.

[27] The late Richard Clearwaters of the Fourth Baptist Church in Minneapolis repeated the assertion, "All ground is level at the foot of the cross," to his large congregation so often, that it is likely every member knew it by heart. He elaborated on this theme in his booklet, *The Local Church of the New Testament* (Minneapolis: Central Press, 1954).

[28] The tandem concept that each local church is sovereign will not be taken up here, but with a later discussion of regional, or hierarchical church government.

[29] See, for example, Clay Nuttall, *The Weeping Church* (Schaumburg, IL: Regular Baptist Press, 1985), 40-47.

[30] Schmidt lists five different synonyms of ἐκκλησία in the Greek language. K.L. Schmidt, "ἐκκλησία" *Theological Dictionary of the New Testament*, III, Geoffrey Bromiley, trans. (Grand Rapids: Eerdmans, 1965), 516.

[31] Ibid., 515-516.

[32] Ibid.

[33] Wolfgang Schrage, "συναγωγή" *Theological Dictionary of the New Testament*, VII, 802-803. See also Edwin Hatch and Henry A. Redpath, *A Concordance to the Septuagint*, 2nd ed. (Grand Rapids: Baker Books, 1998), 433, 1309-1310. Schrage argues that the apostles would have chosen to use ἐκκλησία instead of συναγωγή because 1) συναγωγή had become much more common in NT Judaism than ἐκκλησία. 2) the term "synagogue" had largely lost its universal character, 3) its first reference had become the local building for Jewish worship, and 4) the synagogue was bound up with the Law and the Tradition of the Elders, whereas, the Christian community owed its origin to the Christ event. Schrage, 829.

[34] Richard C. Trench, *Synonyms of the New Testament* (Grand Rapids: Eerdmans, 1978 rprn.), 1-2. Trench goes on to say, "That they were summoned is expressed in the latter part of the word; that they were summoned out of the whole population, a select portion of it, including neither the populace, nor strangers, nor yet those who had forfeited their civic rights, this is expressed in the first." His conculsion, that this has significance for the nature of the Christian church, is now much disputed.

Chapter 1: A defense of Self-Government for the Church

[35] Meaning "assembly, convocation, congregation," BDB, 874.
[36] James Barr, *The Semantics of Biblical Language* (London: SCM Press, 1961), 121.
[37] Ibid., 122.
[38] Ibid., 127-128.
[39] Radmacher, 115.
[40] Millard Erickson, *Christian Theology* (Grand Rapids: Baker, 1985), 1031.
[41] Radmacher, 132. Radmacher's entire chapter on the meaning of the word, *ekklesia* is very thorough, and would aid any reader in understanding the whole issue of the nature of the New Testament Church.
[42] Ibid., 131.
[43] Henry George Liddel and George Scott, *A Greek-English Lexicon*, 9th ed. (Oxford: Clarendon, 1968), 509.
[44] J.Y. Campbell, "The Origin and Meaning of the Christian Use of the Word ΕΚΚΛΗΣΙΑ" *Journal of Theological Studies* 49 (April, 1948), 132.
[45] Simon Hornblower, "Greece: the History of the Classical Period," *The Oxford History of Greece*, John Boardman, Jasper Griffin, and Oswin Murray, Eds. (Oxford: Oxford University, 1986), 156-161.
[46] LSJ, 509. Liddel and Scott cite the assembly of the Spartans referred to in Thucydides. The reference is to an assembly of the Spartans (who practiced an oligarchy), and their allies.
[47] Hornblower, 157.
[48] This is brought out in one instance in the New Testament, in Acts 19:23-41. The following statement also sheds light on how democracy was understood in the Hellenistic world: "Even in the Hellenistic period, i.e. after 322 BC when Athenian democracy in its classical form was suppressed by Macedon, there was . . . more democratic life in Greece (Athens included) than is often realized." "Democracy, non-Athenian and post-Classical," *The Oxford Classical Dictionary*, 3rd ed. Simon Hornblower and Anthony Spawforth, eds. (Oxford: Oxford University, 1996), 454.
[49] Campbell, 132.
[50] "elections and voting," *The Oxford Classical Dictionary*, 3rd ed., 516.
[51] Giles, 25, 182.
[52] Ibid., 9-19.
[53] Ibid., 4-8; 23-25; 230-240.
[54] Ibid., 233-238. Among the later writings of the OT, Giles includes Deuteronomy. To do so, one must overlook the 17 times that Deuteronomy says that Moses spoke or wrote down its contents. It also neglects the five times in the OT that the book of Deuteronomy is attributed to Moses (1 Kings 2:3; 8:53; 2 Kings 14:6; 18:6, 12). Even among critical scholars (i.e., those who do not accept Mosaic authorship), there is no unity as to which writings of the Pentateuch preceded others. See R.N. Whybray, *The Making of the Pentateuch*, JSOT (Sheffield: Sheffield Academic Press, 1987).
[55] Giles, 234-235. He mentions 1QM 4.10 and 1QSa 2.4 as expressing the same meaning.
[56] Schmidt argues that the primary meaning of ἐκκλησία for the church came from the LXX. He does not, however, completely rule out the influence of secular Greek. Schmidt, 14.

[57] See the discussion of Barr, above.

[58] This has to play a role, for the book of Acts was written to an audience with Greek, not Jewish understanding. The *ekklesia* in Acts 19:32-41 needs no explanation. Things like the basic beliefs of the Pharisees and Saducees (23:7-8) do.

[59] Giles' view of the meaning of *ekklesia* is essentially the same as that of T.F. Torrence. Though Giles does not try to base his view on etymology, as Torrence does, he nevertheless gives *ekklesia* the same meaning. It is primarily Torrence's view that Barr was arguing against.

[60] For instance, "all the congregation" – Heb., *qahal* is preceded by 8:1, "And all the people gathered themselves together as one man into the street that was before the water gate." See also four instances he cites as meaning "the covenant community," 1 Kings 8:14,22,55,65; which are preceded by 8:1, "Then Solomon assembled the elders of Israel, and all the heads of the tribes . . . and all the men of Israel assembled themselves unto king Solomon." Most of the instances he cites in Deuteronomy are debatable, the one exception being Deuteronomy 23:1. Here, Giles states, "In these passages, the event of assembling is envisaged, but the author depicts the *qahal* as a theological entity, God's covenant people, the recipients of the law, a defined community set apart to worship Yahweh. In other words, *qahal* in Deuteronomy can be used as a concrete noun to refer to Israel." 233. He also cites Craigie's comment on this passage. However, Craigie's statement does not fully back up Giles' conclusion. Note, "Here the word has general reference to Israel as a worshipping community. Thus to enter the assembly of the Lord would indicate a person who became a true Israelite and who therefore shared in the worship of the Lord. The expression is somewhat narrower in its intent than Israel, taken as a whole, for there would be resident aliens and others, who, though a part of the community, were nevertheless not full members of it." P.C. Craigie, *Deuteronomy*, NICOT (Grand Rapids: Eerdmans, 1976), 296.

[61] Giles, 236.

[62] Ibid., 233.

[63] Barr, 122.

[64] See BDB, 417.

[65] Ibid.

[66] Ibid., 874.

[67] Jack P. Lewis, "עדה," in *Theological Wordbook of the Old Testament* (1980). Lewis points out that the use of *edah* in Psalm 82:1 is nearly identical to the Ugaritic equivalent denoting the assembly of the gods of the Canaanite pantheon.

[68] Barr points out that at least three matters enter into this discussion: 1) which Hebrew word was used by Hebrew writers at different times, 2) which Greek translation was used for these words in rendering the Bible into Greek, and 3) which words (whether Hebrew, Aramaic or Greek) were used for a place of worship by the Jews at various times. Barr, 128. Schmidt commends the conjecture that the LXX translators used ἐκκλησία for the Heb. קהל on account of the similarity of sound. In my estimation, Giles does not effectively deal with these three issues when coming to his conclusions. His excursis never really gets away from the dialectic of maximum theological content (the covenant community), versus minimum theological content (assembly).

[69] F.A.J. Hort, *The Christian Ekklesia* (London: McMillan, 1914).

[70] Robert A. Baker, "An Introduction to the Study of the Development of Ecclesiology." (unpublished dissertation, Southwestern Baptist Theological Seminary, 1944)

[71] Radmacher, 129.

[72] Ibid., 131.

[73] Barr, 129.

[74] Though not directly related to the nation of Israel, it is interesting that the earliest form of government in Mesopotamia yet discovered was a democratic type, among the Sumerians. This government had a bicameral assembly, which made decisions for the good of the community. Walter Bodine, "The Sumerians," *Peoples of the Old Testament World,* Alfred J. Hoerth, Gerald Mattingly and Edwin M. Yamauchi, Eds. (Grand Rapids: Baker, 1994), 22.

[75] Gedaliah Alon, *The Jews in their Land in the Talmudic Age,* Gershon Levi, trans. (Jerusalem: Magnes Press, 1980), 177-179.

[76] Salo Wittmayer Baron, *A Social and Religious History of the Jews,* Vol. II (New York: Columbia University, 1957), 75. This is reflected in the description of David's anointing as King by the assembly of the elders of Israel, who represented the entire nation (1 Chronicles 11:1-3).

[77] Radmacher points out that these modifiers were used by Paul especially in the early phase of his missionary ministry. 136-138.

[78] Ibid., 139.

[79] John MacArthur, Jr., *Answering Key Questions about Elders,* n.p. 1984, 21. His argument runs as follows: first, the choice was not of elders, but of "servants." Second, "The people brought them to the Apostles for approval – not the reverse (v.6). The congregation recognized these men as godly and qualified men, but the Apostles appointed them to their task." MacArthur misses the point. Apostolic approval does not eliminate congregational choice. Asking for parental approval of a marriage (which many young couples in western culture still do) does not nullify the fact that the primary "choosing" was done by the young man and young woman, not the parents. MacArthur believes that it is the duty of the elders to appoint deacons, 13.

[80] Mal Couch, ed. *A Biblical Theology of the Church* (Grand Rapids: Kregel, 1999),185.

[81] See BAGD, where ἐπισκέπτομαι here, is defined as "look at, examine, inspect." 298.

[82] The word ἐπισκέπτομαι occurs over 140 times in the LXX, and is most often used to translate the Hebrew פקד, meaning, "number, muster" and less frequently, "visit." See Edwin Hatch and Henry A. Redpath, *A Concordance to the Septuagint,* 2nd ed. (Grand Rapids: Baker, 1998), 527-528. Both Jesus (Mt. 25:35f) and James (Ja. 1:27) used the word to mean "look after." Beyer states that "to appoint to an office," is the meaning of this word in Acts 6:3, and that the Numbers 27:3 passage was perhaps a guide for the Apostles in this action. Beyer, "ἐπισκέπτομαι," TDNT, II, 603-605.

[83] Xenophon used the term ἐκλέγω to mean "*pick out* the best rowers from the fleet." (in this case, it was for a difficult task that had to succeed). Herodotus uses it to describe the rational choice of which customs to adopt as one's own. LSJ, 511.

[84] As Decker points out, "The congregational involvement is evident in the implementation of this solution recorded in Acts 6:5: ἤρεσεν ὁ λόγος ἐνώπιον παντὸς τοῦ πλήθους "the word pleased the whole assembly." Rodney J. Decker, "Polity and the Elder Issue," *Grace Theological Journal,* 9.2 (Fall, 1988), 273. See also the discussion

of grammar and vocabulary in Steven Spencer, *The Portrait of Philip in Acts,* JSNOT (Sheffield: University of Sheffield, 1992), 196.

[85] *A Biblical Theology of the Church,* 185.

[86] Hermann W. Beyer, "ἐπισκέτομαι," TDNT, II, 605.

[87] Ronald Y.K. Fung, "Ministry in the New Testament," *The Church in the Bible and the World,* D.A. Carson, Ed. (Grand Rapids: Baker, 1987), 164.

[88] For this translation of ἔστησαν, see BAGD, 382.

[89] F. Scott Spencer, *The Portrait of Philip in Acts,* JSONT (Sheffield: University of Sheffield, 1992), 197.

[90] BAGD, 382. Note how the word is used in the same way in Acts 6:13 in the court case against Stephen. The group of men that were against him "put forth" false witnesses.

[91] Oswyn Murray, "Liberty and the Ancient Greeks," *The Good Idea: Democracy in Ancient Greece,* John A. Koumoulides, Ed. (New Rochelle: Caratzas, 1995), 35.

[92] Simon Kistenmaker, *Acts* (Grand Rapids: Baker, 1990), 68.

[93] See for instance J. Vernon McGee, *Through the Bible with J. Vernon McGee,* IV: *Matthew-Romans* (Pasadena: Through the Bible Radio, 1983), 514-515. Clayton Nuttall believes that Peter was "operating fully in the flesh," Clayton L. Nuttall, *The Weeping Church* (Schaumberg: Regular Baptist Press, 1985), 42-43.

[94] Kistenmacker, 68.

[95] J.B. Lightfoot and J.R. Harmer, *The Apostolic Fathers: Greek Texts and English Translations,* 2nd ed. Michael W. Holmes, ed. (Grand Rapids: Baker, 1992), 25.

[96] Ibid., 79.

[97] Nuttall states, "Certainly a form of democratic expression is in sight here." But he is insistent that no vote was taken. Clay Nuttall, *The Weeping Church* (Schaumberg: Regular Baptist Press, 1985), 115. He regards voting as a false principle in a church, 43-44. One wonders, however, how hundreds of people would express their approval of a decision, plus select representatives ("it pleased the apostles and elders with the whole church") without voting or doing something similar. Nuttall never really makes this clear.

[98] With these points in mind, and those made in the next two paragraphs, it is hard to understand the following statement by MacArthur: "Nothing in Scripture indicates that anyone at a lower level of leadership should be involved in decision making as it relates to church policy or doctrine." MacArthur, 31.

[99] Spencer notes, "Such a procedure (praying/laying on of hands) obviously echoes the Jerusalem community's dealings with the Seven in Acts 6." 198.

[100] Richard N. Longenecker, *Acts* EBC (Grand Rapids: Zondervan, 1981), 416. Bruce, Lenski, and Kistenmacker agree with Longenecker. Knowling argues that this decision did not have to involve the whole church: R.J. Knowling, *The Acts of the Apostles,* EGC, II (Grand Rapids: Eerdmans, 1979 rprn.), 283. His arguments are countered by those of Meyer, written a generation earlier. H.A.W. Meyer, *Commentary on the New Testament,* IV, William P. Dixon, trans. (Winona Lake, IN: Alpha Publications, 1979 rprn.), 245n.

[101] MacArthur argues that the choice was probably done by representative leaders of churches. MacArthur, 21. This helps harmonize the passage with his view. Though

possible, the explanation is speculative, and no precedent for the assumed process can be established from the New Testament.

[102] BAGD, 881.

[103] Eduard Lohse, "χειροτονέω" TDNT, IX, 437.

[104] Lightfoot and Holmes, *Apostolic Fathers,* "Ignatius to the Philadelphians," 10.1; "Ignatius to the Smyrnaeans," 11.2; "Ignatius to Polycarp," 7.2.

[105] "Accordingly, there is in almost every city a storehouse for the sacred things to which it is customary for the people to come and there to deposit their first fruits, and at certain seasons there are sacred ambassadors selected on account of their virtue, who convey the offerings to the temple. And the most eminent men of each tribe are elected to this office, that they may conduct the hopes of each individual safe to their destination; for the lawful offering of the first fruits are the hopes of the pious." Philo, *De Specialibus Legibus,* I.78 from, *The Works of Philo,* E.D. Yonge, trans. (Peabody: Hendrickson, 1993), 541.

[106] B.F. Westcott, *The Epistles of St. John* (Grand Rapids: Eerdmans, 1982 rprn.), 139.

[107] James Denney, *Studies in Theology* (Grand Rapids: Baker, 1976 rprn.), 189. This quote from Denney is made with reference to the universal church, but can be equally applied to the local church.

[108] Iranaeus, *Against Heresies,* III.3 *The Ante-Nicene Fathers,* Vol. 1 (Peabody: Hendrickson, 1994 rprn.), 415-416.

[109] Tertullian, *The Prescription Against Heretics,* III. ANF, 258.

[110] *Catechism of the Catholic Church* (New York: Doubleday, 1995), 254.

[111] Hans Küng, *The Church,* Ray and Rosaleen Ockenden (Tunbridge Wells: Search Press, Ltd, 1968), 125.

[112] Alexander Rattray Hay, *The New Testament Order for Church and Missionary* (Audobon: New Testament Missionary Union, 1947), 51.

[113] Karsten Burgener argues that this simply means that in the third stage the church carries out the sentence made by the clergyman. He bases his interpretation on the action of Israel in Numbers 15:33-34. Karsten Burgener, *Amt und Abendmahl* (Bremen: Selbstverlag, 1985), 23.

[114] BAGD, 688. NASB, NIV, NRSV. Likewise C.F.D. Moule, *An Idiom Book of New Testament Greek* (Cambridge: Cambridge University, 1959), 108. See also usage of πλέων in Acts 19:32; 1 Cor. 15,1.

[115] James Lightfoot, *St. Paul's Epistle to the Philippians* (Grand Rapids: Zondervan, 1953 rprn.), 198.

[116] Philip E. Hughes, *The Second Epistle to the Corinthians* NIC (Grand Rapids: Eerdmans, 1962), 66.

[117] P.T. Obrien, "Church," in *Dictionary of Paul and His Letters* (Downers Grove: InterVarsity, 1993), 131.

[118] Deckert, 276.

[119] William Hendricksen, *The Gospel of Matthew* (Grand Rapids: Baker, 1973), 701.

[120] Emil Schurer, *The History of the Jewish People in the Age of Jesus Christ,* II, revised ed. Geza Vermes, Fergus Millar and Matthew Black, eds. (Edinburgh: T & T Clark, 1979), 431.

[121] Clearly, this does not hold true in every case. The "Anti-missionary movement" in the United States is an example of Baptist (thus congregational) churches which opposed evangelism.

[122] *Catechism of the Catholic Church* (New York: Doubleday, 1995), 252. I.9.4.1.

[123] See Kenneth Scott Latourette, *A History of the Expansion of Christianity* (New York: Harper, 1937), 116-117.

[124] D. James Kennedy, *Evangelism Explosion* (Wheaton: Tyndale, 1977), 3-4.

[125] Burgener, a conservative Lutheran, for instance, argues that there is no trace of anything democratic in the Bible. Instead, one finds an "absolute Lord-servant-relationship." (absolute Herr-Knechte-Verhältnis). Those appointed by Jesus to lead have his same authority over the disciples. *Amt und Abendmahl*,17. Burgener rejects the doctrine of the priesthood of the believer, and admits that his views are at variance in some instances, with those of Luther, 61.

[126] James Lightfoot, "The Christian Ministry," *St. Paul's Epistle to the Philippians* (Grand Rapids: Zondervan, 1953 rprn.), 240.

[127] Epistle LXVIII.8. Alexander Roberts and James Donaldson, eds. *ANF*, 5, 374-375.

[128] See, for example, Epistle LV.1, *ANF*. 5, 347.

[129] Epistle XLV.3 *ANF*.5, 323.

[130] W.C.H. Friend, *The Rise of Christianity* (Philadelphia: Fortress, 1984), 403.

[131] Edward Gibbon, *The Decline and Fall of the Roman Empire*, Vol. I (New York: Random House, n.d.), 430.

[132] "The Apostolic Constitutions, II" xxv. *ANF*, 7, 409. "The bishop, he is the minister of the word, the keeper of knowledge, *the mediator between God and you* in the several parts of your divine worship. He is the teacher of piety; and, *next after God, he is your father,* who has begotten you again to the adoption of sons by water and the Spirit. He is your ruler and governor; *he is your king and potentate; he is, next after God, your earthly god,* who has a right to be honoured by you." xxvi (410) (Italics added).

[133] Ray C. Steadman, "A Pastor's Authority," Discovery Papers (nr. 3500), © 1976 RCS All rights reserved.

[134] Kenneth O. Gangel, *Feeding and Leading* (Grand Rapids: Baker, 1996), 90.

[135] These elements of public worship essentially agree with those of the synagogue in the time of Paul. See Emil Schurer, *The History of the Jewish People in the Age of Jesus Christ*, Vol. II, Geza Vermes, Fergus Millar and Matthew Black, eds. (London: T&T Clark, 1979), 447-454.

[136] Fee states, "Like all the former lists in these chapters, this final one is *ad hoc*; it is intended neither to give the 'order' of service nor to be exhaustive of what 'each one has' to offer by way of minstry." Gordon Fee, *The First Epistle to the Corinthians* (Grand Rapids: Eerdmans, 1987), 690.

[137] Leon Morris, "Church Government," *Evangelical Dictionary of Theology,* Walter Elwell, ed. (Grand Rapids: Baker, 1984), 239. Gilbert Kirby states, in a similar way, that Congregationalism "may be traced back to the reign of Queen Elizabeth I." "Congregationalism," *New International Dictionary of the Christian Church*, 2nd ed. J.D. Douglas, ed. (Grand Rapids: Zondervan, 1978), 251.

[138] Morris, 240.

[139] Estep, 190.

Chapter 1: A defense of Self-Government for the Church   55

[140] "Congregationalism," *The Oxford Dictionary of the Christian Church,* 2nd ed. F.L. Cross and E.A. Livingstone, eds. (Oxford: Oxford University Press, 1990), 332. The arguments for the basic tenets of Congregationalism are found in Luther's tract: "Dass eine christliche Versammlung oder Gemeinde Recht und Macht habe, alle Lehre zu beurteilen und Lehrer zu berufen, ein-und abzusetzen." This tract was written in 1524, before the Peasants' War.

[141] Alexander Strauch, *Biblical Eldership* (Littelton: Lewis and Roth, 1986), viii. A survey of Anabaptist documents on the subject of church leadership shows that they explained the work of the pastor/elder in the same way Strauch describes it. See Walter Klassen, *Anabaptism in Outline: Selected Primary Sources* (Scottdale, PA: Herald Press, 1981), 118-138. Anabaptist churches used the titles: pastor, elder, bishop, preacher, minister, to describe the office. Depending on the needs of the congregation, a church might have one or several bishops (elders). In the 17th and 18th century, Baptist pastors were typically designated as "elders."

[142] Eduard Schweizer, *Church Order in the New Testament,* Frank Clarke, Trans. (London: SCM Press, 1961), 19.

[143] Couch, 185.

[144] Douglas McLachlan, "Who Makes the Decisions at Your Church?" *Baptist Bulletin,* October, 1988, 13.

[145] This, says Burgener, is the weakness of anything democratic. *Amt und Abendmahl,* 19-20.

[146] "From the disorders that disfigure the annals of those republics (of ancient Greece and Rome) the advocates of despotism have drawn arguments, not only against the forms of republican government, but against the very principles of civil liberty. They have decried all free government as inconsistent with order in society, and have indulged themselves in malicious exultation over its friends and partisans." Alexander Hamilton, "The Federalist No. 9" *The Federalist Papers* (New York: Modern Library, n.d.), 48.

[147] Though not mentioning political character, Chuck Smith uses precisely this argument for evaluating congregational government as non-New Testament. "I don't believe that congregational rule is an option because we really never see an example in the Bible where the congregation was right. It was the congregation that was always coming and saying, "We want a king to rule over us like the other nations," making demands that were not after the will of God. I can find no Scriptural example of effective congregational rule. We do read of congregations attempting to rule. In Exodus 16:2 we read, "And the whole congregation of the children of Israel murmured against Moses and Aaron in the wilderness:" Smith then quotes Numbers 14:1-3, 27 and concludes, "So woe to the man who pastors a congregational church. Like Moses, the pastor will only find murmuring and uprisings." Chuck Smith, "Principles of the Calvary Chapel Movement: 2 Church Government" (internet document) http://www.calvarychapel.com/hope/library/smith-chuck/books/ccd/02_church_gov.htm (12/31/03)

[148] BDB, 978 (6).

[149] Couch, 158.

[150] See 1 Cor. 12:13; 2 Cor. 1:22; 1 Jn. 2:18-27.

[151] Herman Ridderbos, *Paul: An Outline of his Theology* John Richard De Witt, trans. (Grand Rapids: Eerdmans, 1975), 473

[152] Nathan Hatch, *The Democratization of American Christianity* (New Haven: Yale University Press, 1989). The perspectives of Hatch and Wells are different on this subject. Hatch presents the story of the changes in American Protestant religion (as well as the rise of the Mormon religion) after the American War for Independence. He objectively evaluates the positives and negatives of the great changes which took place. This often includes high praise for much that the Baptists, Methodists, and Disciples of Christ achieved. He likewise relates what was unfortunate and unbiblical. The overall tone is a positive one. For Wells, the story is almost a cause for lament.

[153] David. F. Wells, *No Place for Truth: Or, Whatever Happened to Evangelical Theology?* (Grand Rapids: Eerdmans, 1993), 205-207.

[154] Robert Browning, "How Democratic was Ancient Athens?" *The Good Idea: Democracy in Ancient Greece,* 65.

[155] It is, however, correct that many of the leading preachers of the more democratic American denominations during the first half of the nineteenth century placed too much faith in human reason and goodness. Hatch, 163. The rationalism of these men, however, is of a different kind than that of other American religious leaders, such as Charles Chauncy, Samuel Quincy, and William Ellery Channing. Their rationalism led them to reject the doctrines of the Trinity, the inherent sinfulness of man, and the Atonement. H. Shelton Smith, Robert T. Handy, and Lefferts A. Loetscher, *American Christianity: An Historical Interpretation with Representative Documents,* Vol. I (New York: Schribners, 1960), 374-414; 481-517.

[156] Hatch, 125-161.

[157] Alexis de Tocqueville, *Democracy in America,* 13th ed. J.P. Mayer, Ed. (New York: Harper and Row, 1969), 542.

[158] Arnold J. Toynbee, *A Study of History,* Vol. IV (Oxford: Oxford University Press, 1957), 370.

Chapter 2

Making the Self-Government of the Local Church Function Well

Even if church leaders have an excellent understanding of what the Bible teaches about church government, their church can still wind up being an unstable boiling pot. The church is more than a decision-making assembly. She is a fellowship, a body, an evangelistic team, a spiritual temple and a family that offers acceptance to its members and to outsiders that are open to its message. In order for self-government to function correctly in a local church, several factors must be present.

Individual Voice

Every member of a local church has the right to recommend candidates for various ministries or functions (e.g. elders, deacons). The mind of the membership also needs to be sought for matters like buildings or church discipline. The Reformed theologian, William Hendricksen, writes that there are two extremes which have developed in some groups in modern times. The first extreme is the minimizing of the authority of church leadership. The second is

> ... the extreme of belittling the high standing, in the eyes of God, of the entire congregation, as if it lacked maturity; as if the body of all believers, whether conceived locally ... denominationally, or universally, had no real "say" in matters of discipline or otherwise; and as if it were the privilege of the ecclesiastical authorities to rule arrogantly, as so many "little tin gods" ....[1]

Particularly among independent churches this second error is on the increase. Without disputing their high spiritual motivation, many church leaders seek a system of organization that eliminates the average member from the church decision-making process. The action is in fact understandable, since many pastors and church leaders are frustrated with church squabbles over unimportant issues. But this kind of answer to the problem is incorrect. To establish a system that eliminates the members from the decision-making (as, for instance, to eliminate all congregational voice in the choice of elders) is simply a new form of hierarchy.

But the exercise of individual voice also needs to be limited. A preacher must preach the message God has given him, not what the congregation chooses. Otherwise he steps out of the role of God's messenger. Peter never asked the church whether he should accuse Ananias of lying to the Holy Spirit (Acts 5:1-10). God's message is often painful. Likewise not every ministry in the local church is an elected ministry: Sunday school teachers need to be selected by the elder, deacon or superintendent in charge. Only ministers responsible to the whole congregation need to be chosen by the whole congregation.[2]

Perhaps this is the correct place to point out how church-wide decisions are limited to church-wide matters. If the church has given someone a responsibility (and sometimes that is simply a matter of asking "Who is willing to do this?") then the church must also give that person the accompanying authority. If children's church workers have a question about what to put on the bulletin board, or what the routine should be, that is a matter properly settled among themselves, or by the leader of the children's church ministry. If the same workers have a question about what kind of literature should be used, they should clear that with a pastor (or someone designated by a pastor), since the spiritual direction of the church is his particular ministry. If a children's church worker teaches false doctrine, that is a matter taken care of by stages of church discipline. In his discussion of spiritual gifts in Romans 12:3-8, Paul teaches that every Christian needs to be active and self-motivated in his or her service to the other brethren. Active, self-motivated ministers must operate within the bounds set upon them by the Word of God and the local church. But they need to likewise be set free to work within those bounds.

Individual Responsibility

The second requirement for a healthy self-government of the local church is more difficult to fulfill than the first. Hebrews 10:24-25 states that every believer has the responsibility to admonish his neighbor to live a life of love and good works. If a Christian observes his brother going a false direction, he needs to correct him in love. From Romans 12, 1 Corinthians 12 and 1 Peter 4:10-11 we learn that every believer should be doing a ministry in the church: "As each one has received a special gift, employ it in serving one another, as good stewards of the manifold grace of God" (1 Pet. 4:10). A church does not consist of two servants and 100 overseers; rather every member needs to do his work.

Joseph Stowell, III relates that during his pastorate in Detroit, the church determined to add a pastor for singles' ministries to the staff. He goes on to say that this proposal ran into resistance from some of the older people in the church:

> Their question was insightful and difficult to field. According to them, in the late thirties and forties the church was running fifteen hundred persons in Sunday school and yet the church had only two pastors. "Why," they asked, "do we need so many pastors today?" The reality of it was that the church was planted in a time when the work ethic was valued in America . . . Immigrants from the old country had come to work in the automobile factories with a sense of the importance of their work and contribution. When they went to the factory, they planned to participate and give of themselves as much as they could. When they came to church, they came the same way – walking in with that "what-can-I-do-to-help" attitude."[3]

This kind of attitude no longer holds sway on either side of the Atlantic. Stowell relates the story to help pastors understand that they will have to deal with this phenomenon. But Christians in general need to grapple with this problem as well. The life and success of the church depends on them, not just on the pastor. All lasting church work demands sacrifice.

Strong Leadership

In every spiritual movement, leadership plays a decisive role. Every spiritual awakening in church history has also been accompanied by a special enabling of a leader or leaders by the Holy Spirit. Sanders comments, "The church has always prospered most when it has been blessed with strong, spiritual leaders who expected and experienced the touch of the supernatural in their service."[4] Radmacher points out that

> ... not only is the local church a temple of the Holy Spirit in which each member exercises the privileges of a believer-priest, but it is also a flock in which the members submit to the rulership of the undershepherds, who are responsible to the Chief Shepherd for their souls.[5]

Paul even teaches that there is a spiritual gift of leadership for the church in 1 Corinthians 12:28.[6] Beyer states that, "The reference can only be to the specific gifts which qualify a Christian to be a helmsman to his congregation."[7]

Without leadership, the self-government of the church becomes a haystack of contradictory ideas. Without leadership, most of what the church does will be ineffective. Without really intending to, Kenneth Gangel has created a pungent maxim describing this phenomenon: "Good programs administered by poor leaders will fail while even poor programs administered by good leaders can succeed."[8] James Derscham, who worked for the Regular Baptist Press, once related in a seminar that he had been the guest speaker at a particular church. It happened that this church had a business meeting just before he was to speak. As the meeting began, the secretary explained with embarrassment that she had forgotten the business meeting notes at home. The pastor responded, "Well folks, what shall we do, shall we conduct the meeting without notes, or shall we wait until she retrieves the notebook and returns? Let's take a vote on it!" Derscham commented, "This church isn't going anywhere because it doesn't have any leadership." Churches need pastors with the courage to make decisions.

Leadership is a requirement for any spiritual development of a group. But spiritual leadership doesn't appear overnight. Unfortunately many churches or church ministries overlook this truth. Not understanding the necessity of time in leadership development is detrimental to local churches because leadership is a key to stability and growth. Even the apostle Paul, with his calling from the Lord, his unique abilities, and his unsurpassed knowledge of the Scriptures, had to spend years in spiritual development before he was ready to be a leader in Christian work. Pastors, deacons and Sunday School teachers need to look for potential among others in the church. Not everyone possesses the ability to lead. But those who do demonstrate leadership abilities need to be developed as young workers into leaders. A good many pastors, evangelists, and missionaries began their Christian service in senior citizens' homes, children's churches or city missions. On occasion, a pastor notices a Christian is an effective organizer. He needs to give him tasks that require organizing. Pastors and deacons will be chosen by the congregation for their ministries, but when there is no process for leadership development within the local church, there won't be any candidates for pastor or deacon, either.

The Inspired Scriptures

The self-government of the local church is at the same time the strongest and weakest form of church government. The church doesn't depend upon outward organizations or ecclesiastical structures for her stability and endurance, but rather on the Word of God. Churches can only go the way the Lord intends them to go through their study of the Bible (Jn. 15:3). All major decisions that are made by the people of the church together need to have their bases in the Scriptures. This is more true now than at any time in history. Taking up this theme, Philip Ryken says, "The only church that will survive in post-Christian times is a church with a passion for God's Word."[9] For this reason, pastors need to preach God's Word boldly and consistently. They need to preach often about the subject of personal evangelism, which is the life's work of every Christian. They need to make the truths about personal holiness plain, as this is the Christian lifestyle. They need to teach how to serve one another, through sermon and example, as that is where Jesus laid the emphasis for our actions and attitudes (Mk. 10:45; Phil. 2:3-8). Otherwise church members will concentrate too much on themselves and their own problems. Instead of thinking on others, they will clash with one another about unimportant subjects or aggravations. Above all, pastors need to preach about God's nature,[10] and about the Person and Work of Jesus Christ. He is the head of the church. In the beginning of his book, *The Knowledge of the Holy,* A.W. Tozer writes, "The history of mankind will probably show that no people has ever risen above its religion, and man's spiritual history will positively demonstrate that no religion has ever been greater than its idea of God."[11] If this is true, then the logical conclusion is also true: no church can ever rise above its concept of God.

It is significant that the New Testament epistles, which contain major amounts of doctrinal instruction, were most often addressed to the entire local church, and were to be read to and further explained to the whole assembly (Col. 1:16; Heb. 13:22). According to the New Testament pattern, thorough Bible teaching is not to be reserved for the Elders, or a select group of the local assembly, but is to be given to all. If there were ever a time to emphasize this point, it is now. The average unbeliever in America 200 years ago knew more of the Bible than the average member of an evangelical church does today. Daniel Wallace contends, "We are a generation away from biblical illiteracy on a scale that mirrors the middle ages."[12]

Wrong motivations always bring errors into the church. Some churches emphasize projects ahead of their relationship to other Christians or to the Holy Spirit himself. Sometimes Elders have the notion that their first responsibility is to get as many people as possible into the church. This is to put people or results ahead of Gospel truth. This is not a new phenomenon. In the third and fourth centuries AD, many churches made Christianity acceptable by changing pagan gods and demigods of a locale into saints. For example, "At Siena the Temple of Quirinus became the Church of St. Quirino and thus a pagan god was given the Christian canonization."[13] Gregory Thaumaturgos, who evangelized very successfully in Pontus in the third century, AD, instituted festival days to celebrate various martyrs instead of heathen gods and heroes. Because of persecution, he felt this would make the Christian faith easier to accept and more joyful to the unlearned.[14] "The cult of the martyrs," says Harnack, "took over the place of the old local heathen cults with intoxicating, heathen celebration."[15] Instead of destroying pagan temples, missionaries in sixth century England converted them into Christian churches and substituted the worship of relics for the worship of idols. This, says Philip Schaff, "no doubt facilitated the nominal conversion of England, but swept a vast amount of heathenism into the Christian church, which it took centuries to eradicate."[16] There was then and is now plenty of teaching in the New Testament to steer highly-motivated pastors and missionaries away from this kind of error (for instance the instruction in 1 & 2 Timothy). It needs to be heeded. Politicians speak of one generation piling up debts that must be paid by their children or grandchildren. While they might use the idea to get political mileage, in the realm of church work the problem is very real: the errors of one generation become the burdens of those following.

Many churches avoid speaking directly about sin, the blood of Christ or heaven and hell, so as to offend the least number of visitors. When they do so they quit emphasizing the Christ of the Bible, and the harvest reaped will be strictly earth-related (1 Cor. 3:10-15). Paul, like Jesus himself, made the fellowship of the believers on earth a narrow one:

> For though there be that are called gods, whether in heaven or in earth, (as there be gods many and lords many) But to us there is but one God, the Father, of whom are all things, and we in him; and one Lord Jesus Christ, by whom are all things, and we by him. (1 Cor. 8:5-6 KJV)

The early Christian apologists maintained this same approach of the apostles. One is struck when reading the writings of Justin Martyr, Tertullian, Athenogoras, and Minucius Felix how frequently they quoted Scripture, pointed out the ignoble, sinning condition of the human race, preached a crucified and resurrected savior and warned of a literal, burning hell as they addressed their learned heathen counterparts. This is the Christian faith that was so powerfully enduring in its first three centuries that the Roman emperors finally made peace with it, since they knew they could never destroy it.

The self-governing church only functions well if its members are a well-taught, Bible-reading congregation. The Bible was not simply written to tell men how to get to heaven, it was also written to explain to churches how to conduct themselves, what their motivations, responsibilities and restrictions are. The Bible is the rulebook for the church (Phil. 3:15-19; 1 Tim. 3:14-15). Said another way by Radmacher, "Local Christian congregations are only likely to walk more worthily of their high calling if they first learn from Scripture itself more of the ways in which God Himself intends for them to function."[17] Nor should the practical benefits of biblical preaching be overlooked. Earl Comfort surveyed the members of his church in Lincoln Park, New Jersey, which had grown from 300 to 1200 in attendance over a period of 10 years. He found out that though the preaching was not an important factor in attracting people to the church, it was the main factor in keeping people at the church.[18]

Good Organization

Every local church is unique. This uniqueness arises in part from its ethnic composition, its surrounding neighborhood and city, but also mainly from its leaders and members. In the early church there were no Sunday schools, no choirs with songbooks, no church buildings, no tents for evangelistic crusades, no overhead projectors, no Christian videos, no missionary pilots, no youth camps and no children's churches (with puppets, flannelgraphs, teachers' handbooks, etc). But any church which opposes all these methods of communicating and organizing will do very little for Christ. The moment a church is determined to work for Christ, she will need organization. The local church needs organization because "the church is clearly an organization if the words of our language mean anything."[19] Even worship needs organization. Paul told the Corinthian believers, "Let everything be done decently and in order."

In Exodus 18 Jethro observed that Moses was trying to do all the work for the nation of Israel, and said to him, "The thing that you are doing is not good. You will surely wear out, both yourself and these people who are with you; for the task is too heavy for you; you cannot do it alone" (vv.15-16). Next Jethro explained to Moses how to organize his people. Schofield brusquely criticizes this plan with the words, "Jehovah entirely ignored this worldly-wise organization, substituting His own order" (In Num. 11). But the Bible offers no criticism of Jethro's advice. The apostles had a similar problem in the early years of the church in Jerusalem (Acts 6).[20] The solution to the problem was to organize the people. Jesus needed organization to feed 5000 and had the men sit in groups of a hundred or fifty (Mk. 6:39-40). Four centuries after the expansion of the family of Aaron, David organized its priests into 24 orders for service in the temple (1 Chron. 24:1-19). Organization is praised, not criticized in the Bible. Evidence in the New Testament for organization of the church is, as Rolland McCune points out, abundant.[21] After listing 16 examples or commands of organization and/or orderliness in the New Testament, Radmacher concludes, "As a representation of the church universal, the body of Christ, each local church should have the symmetry, the beauty, the decorum, the orderliness characteristic of the archetype."[22]

There are some biblical rules for church organization. There need to be overseers (elders/pastors) and deacons in every church. Activities and worship are to be done in an orderly fashion (1 Cor. 14:40), collections are to be done on Sunday (1 Cor. 16:1-2). But there is much which the Bible simply leaves open: for instance, whether churches must have one or multiple pastors/elders. There are no church committees recorded in the New Testament, but committees can have a very positive, spiritual role in the workings of a church. For this reason one must accept that there is a certain amount of latitude within the limits of Bible directives. As Getz points out, "The Bible is relatively silent regarding organizational and administrative patterns. But this is not without design, for nothing becomes obsolete so quickly as structural forms."[23]

When the New Testament does not specify limits on a function of local church organization, that function can first be formed by the doctrine of the local church. Organization needs to correspond to that doctrine. Otherwise organization will undercut what the church is attempting to achieve. A church that believes it is to be supported by the tithes and offerings of its members, for instance, would be foolish to form a committee for raising church funds through garage sales. Secondly, and in a similar vein, many churches have a mission statement. The organization of the church needs to conform to that mission statement. Directors of ministries or committees that have no connection to the mission of the church will function like excess baggage. They draw down the energies of a body and deflect the group spiritually. Thirdly, organization is established in part by the New Testament description of its ministers. Deacons, for instance, are people who serve (see Chapter 4). The organization of their collective efforts needs to center around service in the church. Finally, principles of wisdom, given for instance in the Book of Proverbs, will set the limits on and give guidelines to organization in a local church. God gives his people wisdom when they seek it (Prov. 2:1-6; Jas. 1:5-8).

Timothy Addington notes, "When it comes to governance, one size does not fit all. There are certain principles that are consistent with good governance across all church sizes, but a church of 100 is not the same as a church of 300, and a church of 300 is not the same as a church of 600."[24] The larger the congregation, the more organization will be necessary. This includes more leaders. People often conceive of church as a worshipful audience listening to a good sermon on Sunday morning. But far more than that is involved in church life, worship and mission. To return to the citation of the feeding of the 5000: Jesus had the disciples organize the people into groups of hundreds and fifties. That was necessary to get all the feeding done: miracle or no miracle. True church life and growth requires not only listening but feedback as well. Personal feedback does not work well in large audiences. The workers in a church need to know how its members are doing. That requires one-on-one conversations. Many times those conversations need to be planned in advance, with appointments. Discipleship itself requires one-on-one contact. One pastor cannot get to all of the people in a church of 100. Ten pastors cannot get to all in a church of 1000. Members of a church are a spiritual work force. The more workers there are in an organization, the more they will need to be organized. This requires the application of principles found throughout the Word of God, rather than supposed "apostolic" structures read into the New Testament.

In his book, *Feeding and Leading*, Kenneth Gangel analyzes the ministry of Nehemiah as an example for Christian leaders. He points out six important principles for organizing oneself and one's work. They are as follows: 1) Organizing serves no end in itself; 2) Organizing should always grow out of need; 3) Organizing depends on decentralization; 4) Organizing should be flexible; 5) Organizing works best with wide participation; 6) Organizing requires records and reports.[25]

Leading a large church according to the teachings of the New Testament is not an impossible task. The twelve apostles managed to lead 10,000 people when the Jerusalem church was at its zenith.[26] The larger the church, the more pastors have to learn and rely on God's wisdom. The example of Solomon is apt for this challenge. Part of the burden in his soul was the size of his nation:

> Now, O LORD my God, you have made your servant king instead of my father David, but I am a little child; I do not know how to go out or come in. And your servant is in the midst of your people whom you have chosen, a great people, too numerous to be numbered or counted. Therefore give to your servant an understanding heart to judge your people, that I may discern between good and evil. For who is able to judge this great people of yours? (1 Ki. 3:7-9, NKJV)

God encourages us to ask him for wisdom (Prov. 2:1-7). His supply is endless.

Good organization requires good communication. Problems arise in the church most often when people do not understand what they are supposed to be doing or what their responsibilities are. Many attempt to do too much, instead of sharing the load with another Christian. Every member in the church needs a clarification of his ministry. Every member needs to know to whom he or she needs to go when there is a question or a problem. Hans Finzel explains:

> Never assume that anyone knows anything. This is a core leadership principle. We can never communicate enough in our organizations. Like the pulsing red cells rushing through our veins keeping our bodies alive, communication systems are the lifeblood of organizations. The folks at the far extremities desperately need to know what is going on in the minds of those at the leadership center, if they are to feel comfortable, safe, and knowledgeable about their work.[27]

An Encouragement of the Use of Spiritual Gifts

One does not have to peruse theological and exegetical books on the subject of spiritual gifts long to find that there is significant difference of opinion about them, without even mentioning charismatic vs. non-charismatic interpretation (the author is decidedly non-charismatic). On the other hand it isn't helpful either to simply brush the away subject.[28] Thom Rainer, following the writing of Greg Ogden, says that

> ... the Reformation never fully delivered on its promise to release all the people of God to do the work of ministry. A clergy/laity dichotomy still exists in the mentality of many churchgoers. For them, the clergy are the doers of the ministry – contrary to the clear biblical teachings that God's people are to do the ministry and works of service (Eph. 4:12).[29]

Radmacher has given the same analysis since the 1970s.[30]

Admonitions about spiritual gifts are found six times in the New Testament (1 Cor. 12, Eph. 4:7-15: 1 Pet. 4:10-11; 1 Tim. 4:14-16; 2 Timothy 1:6-8).[31] The fact that they occur in discussions about local church life and ministry should alert any church leader to their importance. Church life thrives when Christians are applying their spiritual gifts on a regular basis. The church body will inevitably be built up (1 Cor. 12:7). Radmacher states,

Spiritual gifts are the means by which believers are to serve one another in and through the local church. Spiritual gifts are "for the profit of all" (1 Cor. 12:7) by which we teach, encourage, and build up one another. The gifts given by the Holy Spirit are basic to the development of the body of Christ, the church. They are tools in our hands to be used for the benefit of others.[32]

In a much-neglected treatise on the subject of spiritual gifts, the puritan, John Owen, wrote the following, ". . . although the spiritual life of the church doth not consist in them, yet the order and edification of the church depend wholly on them."[33] The Holy Spirit gives gifts not only so that Christians can serve, but also to organize, unite, and perfect the whole body (Eph. 4:7-15).[34]

There are five different lists of spiritual gifts in the New Testament (Rom. 12:5-8; 1 Cor. 12:8-10; 1 Cor. 12:28-30; Eph. 4:11; 1 Pet. 4:10-11). No list is identical to another. Peter's list is simply two broad categories of speaking gifts and serving gifts. James Boyer draws the following conclusion from this phenomenon:

> This would suggest that there is no well-defined list of these grace-gifts of the Spirit. Nor is there any indication in Scripture that the ones named in these five lists are intended to express all of the Spirit's gifts. Instead, we are led to conclude that the Spirit's gifts differ at different times and at different places according to needs.[35]

The reason that the subject of spiritual gifts is important to church government is because gifts and governance are interconnected. As Robert Saucy notes, "The truth that each member of the church is equipped for ministry by the Lord through the Spirit would point again to a certain diffusion of authority throughout the entire church."[36] John McKenzie, commenting on the Spirit gift passages relates them to authority in the following way:

> In the Church the power of authority is identified with the Spirit. The operation of the Spirit is manifest in authority as it is manifest in all the operations of the Church performed by any of its members. The power which authority has is the same

power which each member of the Church possesses; the power is manifested in different works.[37]

This concept of spiritual gifts and church government has to do with a daily governance of the church on a basic level. Believers are to submit themselves to one-another (Eph. 5:21). For example, when a primary Sunday school class goes five minutes overtime, the deacon, whose daughter is sitting inside, waits respectfully outside the door for his little girl until the teacher is finished. Thus, as one believer uses his or her gift in one area of ministry, other believers submit to that believer. Authority for governance is not vested only in a few. Nor is it vested in every member only at a business meeting. It is supposed to be functioning all the time in a church, throughout its membership. Church leaders tend to invent structures for their church and read their creations into the New Testament to give them authority. Their churches would profit more from simple encouragement to serve and submit on the part of everyone.

Unity

Philip Ryken states that, "one unique thing about the church is its diversity. The Christian community is not homogenous, but heterogeneous, consisting of all different kinds of people."[38] But one should not form a wrong conclusion about this truth. The church is not an assembly of differing viewpoints whose primary obligation is to let every idea get a hearing. The pluralistic church of the ecumenical movement is not the New Testament type of church. The church is, instead, a body of people that have believed the Gospel and been baptized in the Holy Spirit. That is the real basis for Christian unity. That is what overcomes the tendencies to divisiveness inherent in a group of diverse people. No church will make spiritual or numerical progress unless it brings the principle of the unity of the body to reality. Luke points out that the first church, which experienced such phenomenal growth, could be characterized as being of "one accord" (or "with one mind, or purpose"[39] Acts 1:14; 2:1, 46; 4:24; 5:12).

Part of church growth strategy of many present-day churches is to make the service especially comfortable for non-Christians, while at the same time downplaying their own convictions. The early church, on the contrary, had very deep-seated convictions which stigmatized them in their society. The evangelists preached eternal life through the acceptance of the Lord Jesus Christ. Their message was "one Lord, one faith, one baptism" (Eph. 4:6). To accept Jesus as Messiah required confession of sin and turning away from the old way of life and thinking (Acts 2:23, 38; 3:14-20; Phil. 3:7; 1 Th. 1:9-10). This faith formed the foundation for the unity of the early church. Any movement away from its basis received strong and swift correction from the apostles (Acts 15:24-29; 1 Cor. 15; Gal 1:6-10; Col. 2:8-23; Rev. 2:12-29).

"To be of one mind" does not mean that no differing viewpoints are allowed. Rather, it means that differing viewpoints are subordinated to the purpose of the Gospel and the testimony of Christ. Paul admonishes Christians, that "All of us who are mature should take such a view of things. And if on some point you think differently, that too God will make clear to you. Only let us live up to what we have already attained. . . . live according to the pattern we gave you" (Phil. 3:15-17 NIV). Christians are "to be of the same mind one to another" (Ro. 15:5). We need one another. Even though we often have to work alone, Christians need a consciousness that together with other members of the church we are "fellow workers for the truth" (3 Jn. 8). Unity of purpose in the local church does not arise from convincing ourselves that we don't have any differences, to repeat: the local church patterned after the New Testament is a diverse group. Nor unity it achieved when differing viewpoints are muzzled, or criticism is disallowed. Such methods or ways of thinking may produce unity, but this kind of unity will only be superficial and typically short-lived. It will not be a unity in the Holy Spirit.

Humility is a necessary ingredient of unity. Humility is best learned by understanding the mind of Christ (Phil. 2:1-8). A second necessary ingredient of unity is openness to one another (Mt. 18:15a). Long-standing conflicts between Christians are always begun or accompanied by the phenomenon of people talking about, instead of with one another. Rather than trying to gain advantage over one another, we need to together seek the mind of the Lord. In terms of church decision-making, that means meeting together to discuss, as well as to decide. Sometimes it means putting off a decision.

Paul also admonished the Christians to "stand firm in one spirit, with one mind striving together for the faith of the gospel" (Phil. 1:27). The word for "striving together," *synathleo,* carries with it the idea of meeting resistance, thus struggling together. It is used either to mean to fight together in a conflict,[40] or to compete together as an athletic team against others.[41] Church members need to determine together what their goals are, rather than each member trying to push through his or her own agenda or favorite doctrines. The forming of parties in a church is contrary to the teaching of the New Testament, because the church only has one head (1 Cor. 3:1-9). The life of the church will always include conflict, but a church will only successfully go through conflicts when it correctly identifies the enemy (namely, Satan and his servants), instead of viewing the other brethren as "the enemy."

Prayer

As Jesus lived among them on earth, the apostles sensed painfully their lack of understanding about prayer (Lk. 11:1). After his resurrection, they clearly understood the truth of uniting prayer with faith, and taught the same to the early church. Before the church took a new direction or began a new ministry, they preceded it with prayer (Acts 4:23ff; 6:6; 13:3). The life and work of the church is spiritual activity. We can do nothing without Christ (Jn. 15:5). All spiritual work is the work of God done in us through the Holy Spirit (Jn. 14:8-14). Andrew Murray describes the principle this way, "The law of the divine working is unchangeable – God's work can only be done by God himself."[42] For this reason Christians need to have God's mind about every new ministry.

United prayer is one way of understanding God's will. When church leaders want to bring something new into the Church, it is crucial that they first pray together until they are united. Their recommendation to the church will be much more effective after much prayer than without prayer. Jesus taught the disciples to pray, wait, then act (Jn. 14-16; Lk. 24:46-49). This they did from the very beginning of the church (Acts 1:8-2:1). The typical pattern of Christians is to act, then pray. Genuine prayer is humbling. It is not a method of preaching to everyone else or a means of subduing everyone else. It is God's prescribed method of communication with Himself, and automatically draws his children closer to him. Genuine sustained prayer causes Christians to drop a lot of egotism, pig-headedness and cherished objectives by the wayside in order to draw closer to their heavenly Father. When church members together draw closer to the Father, they will likely have a better, more unified concept of what to do to achieve God's work.

Grace and Forgiveness

A church that has existed for two years will not be perfect; neither will a church that is 100 years old. Christians are made righteous through the blood of Christ, but they remain sinners here on earth. Either because of youth or lack of spiritual growth, many Christians are immature. The possibility for wrong decisions is therefore present in every church. There are instances where a lot of time has to pass before a church is ready for a new ministry. James recommended, "Be patient therefore . . . do not complain brethren, against one another" (James 5:7-9). Patience is a part of the fruit of the Spirit (Gal. 5:22). Sometimes church leaders attempt to introduce a new form of church government or organization into the body. They begin with high hopes that this new form of organization will solve the main problems of the church; a short while later, a church division takes place and many of the members leave. Even when there is no significant division, Christians often notice a few years later that they have the same problems they had before. Goodness in the church is far more dependent on grace than on government.

Christians need to learn to forgive (Eph. 4:32). That means forgive pastors, forgive deacons, forgive the missions committee, forgive the choir director. Leaders need to learn to forgive the whole assembly, and not take some things so to heart, especially when the maturing process seems to take forever. Simply put: all church leaders, all church members make mistakes; they are a forgiven people and they need to practice forgiveness with one another.

Recommended for Further Study

J. Oswald Sanders. *Spiritual Leadership*. Chicago: Moody, 1998. (Sanders' book, based on his wide experience and study, was first published over 30 years ago. It is a time-tested "must read" for Christian leaders.)

Gangel, Kenneth. *Feeding and Leading*. Grand Rapids: Baker, 1989. (Gangel is an expert among evangelicals in teaching principles of Christian leadership. This book is particularly helpful for local church leaders. Pastors often have difficulty knowing how to turn over authority to others and working with groups. Among other matters contained in the book, Gangel handles this pastoral problem at length, so that by taking his advice, a pastor can feel competent in working with groups and delegating responsibility.)

Finzel, Hans. *The Top Ten Mistakes Leaders Make*. Colorado Springs: Cook Communications, 2000. (A very practical book that makes church leadership understandable to master. The reader will inevitably find himself among the mistake-makers in at least some of the chapters.)

Getz, Gene. *Sharpening the Focus of the Church*. Chicago: Moody, 1986. (Contains much helpful, wise information about church leadership.)

Stowell, Joseph M. *Shepherding the Church*. Chicago: Moody, 1997. (Written by a preacher who has learned to respond well to the difficult pressures of a large ministry. One is sometimes astonished by the behavior—both positive and negative—of leading people in churches and organizations. Stowell offers the reader excellent counsel in how to respond wisely to both pressures and people. He explains the essence of pastoral leadership. His chapter on "Leading Through Loving" is both convicting and encouraging and will greatly aid any man in the pastorate.)

Hughes, Kent and Barbara. *Liberating Ministry from the Success Syndrome*. Wheaton: Tyndale, 1987. (This book has enjoyed continued appeal. It will help a pastor attain exactly what is written in the title.)

Ryken, Philip Graham. *City on a Hill: Reclaiming the Biblical Pattern for the Church in the 21st Century*. Chicago: Moody, 2003. (Ryken presents a refreshing challenge to church leaders to have churches that are not like the world. As he makes this contrast, Graham defines the church according to Christ and his Word. In that it is different from the world with its pluralistic and self-centered values, the church, practicing truth and love, becomes attractive to searching, alienated, disillusioned individuals living in an increasingly self-serving enviornment. His book covers the major points of local church life.)

Tozer, A.W. *The Knowledge of the Holy*. San Francisco: HarperCollins, 1961. (Tozer was a superb writer and one of the masters of American Evangelical thought. His short book is a classic and highly motivating. It is theology made understandable for the layman, yet full of depth to challenge any theologian. He wrote well about the subject because he knew God. Pastors need to communicate God's greatness to their people. This book will surely help.)

Biehl, Bob. *Master-planning*. Nashville: Broadman and Holman, 1997. (In his book, Bob Biehl deals with how-tos of organization. The author draws from experience both in and outside of local church work.)

Malphurs, Aubrey. *Advanced Strategic Planning: A New Model for Church and Ministry Leaders*. Grand Rapids: Baker, 1997.

Sande, Ken. *The Peacemaker*. Grand Rapids: Baker, 3rd ed. 2003. (This book teaches biblical principles for solving conflicts. Ken Sande describes it as a theology of conflict resolution. Sande, a lawyer, is founder of Peacemaker Ministries and has wide experience in conflict resolution outside the courtroom, including conflict resolution in local churches. Further information and resources may be obtained from: Peacemaker Ministries / 1537 Avenue D, Suite 352 / Billings, MT 59102. Tel. 406-256-1583. Website: http://www.HisPeace.org)

Notes

[1] Hendricksen, *Commentary on Matthew*, 700.

[2] Every church needs to establish its fixed practice of choosing pastors/elders and deacons. In the church of the writer, the selection of elders is done by the elders themselves, then submitted to the church body for approval. There is no choice of one over another by the congregation, but only "yes or no." In most churches where there is only one pastor, this form of selecting a candidate is usually taken over by a pulpit committee. Those who are in disagreement with the self-government of the local church typically make a caricature of the process, calling it political, or "a popularity contest." Those who have been involved in the process can attest that it is nothing of the kind, but rather a painstaking, much prayed-over team effort, which is eventually submitted to the church for approval.

[3] Joseph M. Stowell, *Shepherding the Church* (Chicago: Moody, 1997), 21.

[4] J. Oswald Sanders, *Spiritual Leadership* (Chicago: Moody, 1980), 18.

[5] Radmacher, 354.

[6] In the AV the word is translated, "governments." BAGD gives κυβερνήσεις the meaning "administration" and adds "The plural indicates proofs of ability to hold a leading position in the church." 456. The verb κυβερνάω means to steer a ship, LSJ, 1004.

[7] Herman Wolfgang Beyer, "κυβερνήσις," TDNT, III, 1036. Beyer, however, distinguishes between the office of leader and preacher. At the same time, he says that the gift became the enablement for the overseers and the deacons.

[8] Kenneth Gangel, *Feeding and Leading* (Grand Rapids: Baker, 1996), 255.

[9] Philip Graham Ryken, *City on a Hill: Reclaiming the Biblical Pattern for the Church in the 21st Century* (Chicago: Moody, 2003), 25.

[10] Two helpful and time-tested books for preaching on the nature of God are *The Knowledge of the Holy* by A.W. Tozer and *Knowing God* by J.I. Packer.

[11] A.W. Tozer, *The Knowledge of the Holy* (San Francisco: HarperCollins, 1961), 1.

Chapter 2: Making the Self-Government of the Local Church Function Well 77

[12] Daniel B. Wallace, "What It Takes To Lead The Church," (Internet Document) http://www.bible.org/docs/soapbox/leaders.htm. 1/29/03.

[13] Kenneth Scott Latourette, *A History of the Expansion of Christianity*, Vol. 1 (New York: Harper and Brothers, 1937), 321. Latourette cites a long list of such conversions of personages from pagan deity to Christian saint, 320-321.

[14] Adolf von Harnack, *Die Mission und Ausbreitung des Christentums* 4th ed. (Wiesbaden: VMA Verlag, 1924), 757-758.

[15] Ibid., 758-759.

[16] Philip Schaff, *A History of the Christian Church,* Vol. III (Grand Rapids: Eerdmans, rprn), 34-35.

[17] Radmacher, 338.

[18] Earl V. Comfort, "Is the Pulpit a Factor in Church Growth?" *BibSac* 140.557 (1983), 64-70.

[19] Kenneth O. Gangel, *Feeding and Leading* (Grand Rapids: Baker, 1996), 10.

[20] Gene Getz is one of several who makes this analogy between Moses' difficulty in Exodus 18 and the election of the first deacons in Acts 6. He provides a very helpful analysis of the occasion, and its meaning for church organization. He likewise offers Nehemiah 2 and Acts 15 as examples of how the church should handle organizational problems. Gene Getz, *Sharpening the Focus of the Church* (Chicago: Moody, 1986), 185-191.

[21] McCune lists thirteen different instances of evidence for local church organization in the NT: 1. stated meetings (Acts 20:7; Heb. 10:25) 2. elections (Acts 6:5-6) 3. officers (Phil.1:2) 4) designation of its ministers (Acts 20:17, 28) 5. recognized authority of the local church (Mt.18:17) 6. discipline (1 Cor. 5:4-13) 7. contributions (Ro. 15:26; 1 Cor.16:1-2) 8. letters of commendation (Acts 18:27) 9. registry of widows (1 Tim.5:9; Acts 6:1) 10. uniform customs (1 Cor.11:16) 11. observance of the ordinances (Acts 2:41; 1 Cor.11:23-26) 12. (1 Cor.14:40) 13. qualifications for membership (Mt. 28:19; Acts 2:41,47) Rolland D. McCune, "Systematic Theology III" (Seminary Notes, Allen Park: Detroit Baptist Seminary, n.d.), 92-94.

[22] Ibid., 354.

[23] Gene Getz, *Sharpening the Focus of the Church* (Chicago: Moody, 1986), 185. Said in another way by Timothy Addington, ". . . there is nothing sacred per-se about the structures most churches have in place for leadership. Governance structures, apart from what is clearly spelled out in the New Testament as prescriptive are simply tools that should be designed to empower people and facilitate ministry." Timothy J. Addington, *High Impact Boards,* 2 (Unpublished document, Ch. 12).

[24] Timothy J. Addington, *High Impact Boards,* Ch 4, p.17.

[25] Kenneth O. Gangel, *Feeding and Leading* (Grand Rapids: Baker, 1996), 64-67. To better understand these points, read his chapter, "Organizing Yourself and Your Work."

[26] Spence Sawyer, Assistant Supervisor for the Evangelical Free Church, Midwest Region, points out that as a church increases in size to over a thousand, the voice of the congregation expresses itself primarily in "Strategic Governance." By this, he means the church together decides on matters of choosing ministers, accepting budgets, approving building programs, etc. The "Operating Governance" of the church is given over to individuals who are responsible for daily ministries of the church. Sawyer has observed this in his dealings with several churches ranging size from 1000 to 5000

(Sawyer shared this information with me in a personal telephone call in September, 2003).

[27] Hans Finzel, *The Top Ten Mistakes Leaders Make* (Colorado Springs: Cook Communications, 2000), 115.

[28] "The church from the beginning has been plagued by two opposing extremes in its doctrine of spiritual gifts. From the first, as the Corinthian Epistles bear witness, there was abuse of spiritual gifts. In the course of the history of the church, excesses of the wildest kind are found in relation to this doctrine. On the other hand, there has been an appalling failure to appreciate the importance of spiritual gifts as determining the ministry of the church and as being essential to all its fruitfulness. The proper balance of doctrine is found in the Scriptures, and excesses have been noteworthy in their neglect of what the Scriptures actually teach." John Walvoord, *The Holy Spirit* (Grand Rapids: Zondervan, 1965), 163. For the view that Spiritual gifts existed only in the apostolic age see Larry Dean Pettegrew, *The New Covenant Ministry of the Holy Spirit* (Grand Rapids: Kregel, 2001).

[29] Thom S. Rainer *The Book of Church Growth: History, Theology, and Principles* (Nashville: Broadman and Holman, 1993), 195-196, following Greg Ogden, *The New Reformation: Returning the Ministry to the People of God* (Grand Rapids: Zondervan, 1990).

[30] See, for example, Earl Radmacher, "The Question of Elders," (Portland: Western Conservative Baptist Seminary, 1977), 1-2.

[31] 1 Corinthians 7:7 is not considered here, as it has to do with marrying/not marrying, rather than church or evangelistic ministry.

[32] Earl D. Radmacher, *Salvation* (Nashville: Word, 2000), 178.

[33] John Owen, *The Holy Spirit* (Grand Rapids: Sovereign Grace, 1971 rprn.), 833.

[34] The author is aware that the context of Ephesians 4 deals with the universal body of Christ. However, the actions described are played out in the local church. That is where they are observed.

[35] James Boyer, *For a World Like Ours: Studies in 1 Corinthians* (Winona Lake: BMH Books, 1971), 114. Boyer's five lists include three instead of two in 1 Corinthians 12 and none in 1 Peter 4).

[36] Robert Saucy, "Authority in the Church," in *Walvoord: A Tribute*, Donald K. Campbell, ed. (Chicago: Moody, 1984), 228.

[37] John L. McKenzie, *Authority in the Church* (London: Geoffrey Chapman, 1966), 60.

[38] Ryken, 79.

[39] BAGD, Walter Bauer, F. Wilbur Gingrich and Frederick W. Danker, *A Greek-English Lexicon of the New Testament* (Chicago: University of Chicago Press, 1979), 566.

[40] BAGD, 783.

[41] See Ignatius, *Epistle to Polycarp*, 6.1. J.B. Lightfoot, J.R. Harmer and Michael W. Holmes, *The Apostolic Fathers*, (Greek Texts and English Translations) 2nd ed. (Grand Rapids: Baker, 1992), 198-199).

[42] Andrew Murray, *How to Work for God* (Springdale: Whitaker House, 1983 rprn.), 38.

Chapter 3

Elders and Their Work

On September 13, 1882 the Highland Brigade of the English army marched through the Egyptian desert to engage their enemy at Tel-el-Kebir. Because a night march was required, a naval officer attached to the Brigade offered to lead the force successfully through the desert by his knowledge of the stars. The English attacked at daylight and eventually won the battle. The naval officer was mortally wounded. As he lay dying, he asked General Alison, "I led them right, didn't I?"

Every group of human beings needs leadership. The church needs it as well, since the health of a local church depends on it. The New Testament describes two types of leaders within the church (Acts 6:1; 1 Tim. 3). One group of leaders teaches the Word of God. The other organizes service and help. They are called "servants" or, more commonly, "deacons." There are three titles for the group of leaders who are teachers,[1] Their office and ministry are the subjects of this chapter.

Terms for Church Leaders

John Calvin, in his *Institutes* states, "In giving the name of bishops, presbyters, and pastors indiscriminately to those who govern churches, I have done it on the authority of Scripture, which uses the words as synonymous."[2] This is a correct assessment, as will be pointed out in the following discussion. This particular leadership in the church is an appointed leadership: both by God (Acts 20:28) and by men (Acts 14:23). Though accompanied by spiritual gifting, it is not the same thing.[3]

The word "elder" *presbyteros* is used 19 times in the New Testament for the leader of the local church. It is rather to be expected that the leaders of the local churches would be designated with this title, as it was the same title for leaders in the Jewish community.[4] It was also used among the Greeks and Romans for council members.[5] Glasscock argues that the Jewish idea of elder inherently connotes someone over thirty years of age.[6] But he goes on to add, "To Paul or any other Jew, an official elder was not just an older man. He was also a leader, an adviser who judged and counseled."[7] Not only in Israel, but among ancient peoples in general the age of 30 was accepted as the proper time for taking on the responsibilities of a public office.[8] David Mappes states, however, "When referring to an office or official in the church, the concept of old age was not necessarily included in the word 'elder.'" He footnotes this statement with a series of quotes from Ignatius and Philo, which assert that in their thinking, "elder" did not mean a specific age.[9]

The second term for the church leader is "shepherd" *poimen*. The common translation of this word in modern English is "pastor." This word is only used once in the New Testament for church leadership (Eph. 4:11).[10] The context, likewise, is not one about officially appointed leaders but about gifted men who service churches. Essentially, the word "Pastor," when used of an elder is an outgrowth of an understanding of his ministry. The work of an elder is clarified four times as the work of "shepherding" (e.g. Acts 20:28). In fact, the two times in the Bible that elders are directly addressed about their work, it is summed up as doing the work of a pastor (Acts 20: 28-31 and 1 Pet. 5:1-4). Finally, church leaders in an established community are said to "watch over your souls." Lane explains this as "a commendation of the leaders as men with divinely given pastoral authority and responsibility."[11]

Jesus is called the "good shepherd." Hebrews 13:30 calls Jesus, "the great shepherd." This being the case, it is understandable how the New Testament uses the descriptions of shepherding for church leaders. They are to emulate the pattern of their Savior in looking after his sheep. This concept of emulating Christ as shepherd forms the basis for Peter's whole discussion about elders (1 Pet.5:1-4). MacArthur states,

> Poimen, then, emphasizes the pastoral role of caring and feeding, although the concept of leadership is also inherent in the

Chapter 3: Elders and Their Work 81

picture of a shepherd. The focus of the term *poimen* is on the man's attitude. To be qualified as a pastor, a man must have a shepherd's caring heart.[12]

The third term to designate church leaders is "bishop" or "overseer" *episkopos*. This word is used six times for the office of the church leader. The overseer was one who "looked over all" to observe whether everything was in order. Today the word "bishop" has a purely religious meaning. This was not, however, the case in New Testament times. The term "overseer" in the Greek-speaking world was used for a variety of functions in secular life, including supervisors of a market, women who oversaw young married couples, captains of ships, state officials.[13] Interestingly, "the officer in charge of the Ephesian mint is called *episkopos* in the time of Claudius."[14] The term was also commonly used to denote local officials or officers of societies.[15] In each case, protective care was at the heart of the term.[16] In the Greek Old Testament, God is called *episkopos* (Job 20:29). The term is also used of human leaders (Jud. 9:28; Num. 34:14, 4; Ki. 11:15), including overseers in the temple (4 Ki. 11:18). Beyer points out that the terms "overseer" and "deacon"

> . . . were simple, widely known titles, yet not precisely defined and therefore in their very breadth of meaning capable of a new and specific use. It is worth noting that the Christians chose modest words which did not of themselves raise any spiritual claims.[17]

Hans Küng states, „The question of terminology is far from unimportant in establishing the nature of ecclesiastical office."[18] The early Church did not select the terms elder, overseer and shepherd by accident. There were plenty of words in the Greek language to describe hierarchy as the Church began. The early Christians did not adopt these. Küng lists, for example, *arche, time,* and *telos.* He then goes on to say,

> Why is it that the New Testament obviously avoids using these then current and seemingly obvious terms? Clearly because despite the varieties of area they cover, they have one common factor: all express a relationship of rulers and ruled. And it is precisely this which makes them unusable.[19]

The Three Terms Describe One Person

Although most church groups worldwide divide the leadership of the church into multiple offices (bishops, pastors, elders) many exegetes have demonstrated for over four centuries that the three titles—bishop, pastor and elder—all refer to the same teaching office in the local church. James Lightfoot (Church of England) wrote in his commentary on Philippians, "It is a fact now generally recognized by theologians of all shades of opinion, that in the language of the New Testament the same officer in the church is called indifferently 'bishop' (ἐπίσκοπος) and 'elder' or 'presbyter' (πρεσβύτερος)."[20] As noted earlier, Calvin stated this same position clearly in his *Institutes*.[21] In the first half of the 18th century J.A. Bengel wrote that at the time of Paul's missionary work, "the name *bishops* was not yet customary and distinctively applied: but here it has the meaning which its derivation requires, and applies to all *presbyters*, whose title was a more usual one, from its existence in the Jewish Church."[22] One hundred years later, the Anglican exegete Alford essentially missed no opportunity in the four volumes of his *Greek New Testament* to point out that "bishops" originally were synonymous with "elders." About the same time, the Lutheran August Neander generally regarded as the father of modern protestant historiography, emphasized in his work on the early church that the two words had the same meaning and designated an office in the local church.[23] An example of an exegete in the 20th century who makes this argument is Beyer.[24] But all of these, and a host of others could have looked back over ten centuries to find the same arguments by an exegete. By the time of Jerome, in the 5th century, the offices had already been divided into bishop, priest and presbyter. Nevertheless, he argued that they originally all designated one office.[25] Perhaps the writings of Iranaeus (AD 175) were some of those that influenced Jerome. In his *Against Heresies* he clearly uses the three terms synonymously.[26] Though there are modern scholars who distinguish these terms,[27] one could make a very long list of exegetes who argue they are identical. Here are the reasons why:

First, Paul begins his letter to the Philippians by addressing the whole church "together with the overseers and the deacons" (1:1). It is hardly possible that he would have overlooked a group of officers in that introduction. Second, in Acts 20:17 Luke tells us that Paul summoned the elders of the church of Ephesus to himself. In his discourse he tells them that they are responsible to "shepherd the church of God," over which the Lord had made them "overseers." Only a shepherd (that is the meaning of the word "pastor") can shepherd a flock. Third, Peter likewise instructs the elders to "shepherd the flock of God among you." (1 Pet. 5:2). Fourth, the qualifications of bishops in 1 Timothy 3 are essentially the same as those of elders in Titus 1:5-7. In fact, in the Titus passage, Paul without clarification inserts the word *episkopos* as well. Strauch comments, "All elders . . . must be armed with a knowledge of Scripture and be able to teach, judge, exhort, admonish, shepherd, and defend the flock against false teachers."[28]

The Bible makes it clear, therefore, that the three designations: overseer, elder and pastor all denote the same office (or ministry). This office contains a three-fold responsibility: teaching (1 Tim. 3:2; 5:17), leading (or administering, 1 Tim. 5:17), and watching over the flock (1 Pet. 5:2). It needs to be especially emphasized that the elder must have the ability to teach. That ability is the one qualification that distinguishes the elder from the deacon (Eph. 4:11; 1 Tim. 3:2; Tit. 1:9). "Able to teach" has to mean more than an ability to instruct others individually, as such is the goal of every Christian, and comes with maturity (Heb. 5:12). When Paul talks to Timothy and Titus about the ministry of teaching the Word, he has the whole congregation in view. This therefore must be the meaning of "able to teach." Paul does not say that every elder must be regularly before the congregation, but he must possess this ability. Jefferson said, "No man can be a good pastor who cannot preach, any more than a man can be a good shepherd and fail to feed his flock."[29] Thus he functions in the role of a preacher, whether he is in full time service or not.[30]

Qualifications for the Office

It has already been argued from 1 Timothy 3:3 and from Acts 20:19ff that an elder must have the gift of teaching, whether he often teaches in front of the congregation or not. In 1 Timothy 3:1-7 and in Titus 1:5-9, the rest of the qualifications, with one exception, are qualifications of character. As they are the same for elders as for deacons, they will be taken up in the chapter on deacons. The second non-character qualification is that of sex. Paul tells Timothy that the overseer must be "the husband of one wife" (*mia gunaikos aner*). The identical phrase is used by Paul in Titus 1:6. This Greek expression cannot be made to mean anything other than one of the male sex. To this may be added the injunction of 1 Timothy 2:12, not to "allow a woman to teach or exercise authority over a man." This is not to say that women are never to speak in a church setting, pray out loud, report on church matters, or teach women or children. Paul is giving an instruction about the public teaching role of the elder, teacher, or evangelist.[31]

A third qualification to be mentioned here is maturity (1 Tim. 3:6). One who does not possess this trait and is given the office of elder will likely "become conceited and fall into the condemnation incurred by the devil." Huther notes that the verb translated "become conceited," ". . . comes from *typhos,* which in the figurative sense especially denotes darkness, as beclouding a man's mind so that he does not know himself, so that the consciousness of his own weakness is hidden from him."[32] The highly elevated position of shepherd and spiritual teacher of a congregation is not fitting for a new convert for the simple reason that it will naturally go to his head. It is noteworthy that Paul was not presenting a new concept about leadership. Ancient secular writers voiced the same conviction. Note the following statement by Aristotle about leaders in the political realm:

> But there is another kind of rule – that exercised over men who are free, and similar in birth. This we call rule by a statesman. It is this that a ruler must first learn through being ruled, just as one learns to command cavalry by serving under a cavalry-commander and to be a general by serving under a general, and

by commanding a battalion and company. This too is a healthy saying, namely that it is not possible to be a good ruler without first having been ruled.[33]

Must Elders Be Multiple Or May They Be Single in a Congregation?

Strauch is one of many who believe that a local church must have a plurality of elders in order to function according to the New Testament pattern.[34] MacArthur also strongly emphasizes that there needs to be a plurality of elders in a local church. He writes,

> Clearly, all the biblical data indicates that the pastorate is a team effort. It is significant that every place in the New Testament where the term *presbyteros* is used, it is plural, except where the Apostle John uses it of himself in 2 and 3 John, and where Peter uses it of himself in 1 Peter 5:1. The norm in the New Testament church was a plurality of elders.[35]

However, he also concedes that there may have been churches in New Testament times that had only one elder.[36] Getz takes the position that the New Testament teaches the plurality of elders in a local church, but that some of this may have had to do with the logistics of church life: namely that large churches, such as those in Jerusalem and Ephesus, did not meet in one place.[37] Strauch goes so far as to say that the plurality of elders in Acts 14:23 demonstrates that Paul "established a council of elders in each local church."[38] But the notion of a "council of elders" cannot be proven from the plural of *presbyteros* itself.[39]

Nuttall takes the opposite position, that one cannot argue from the New Testament that there must always a plurality of elders in each church.[40] So does Wagner, who says:

> The argument for many elders in the church based on plurality is not as convincing as it seems on the surface. When Paul said to ordain elders in every city (Titus 1:5), did he mean plurality of elders in every city, or a plurality of elders because there is a

plurality of cities? If every city had one pastor, and there were many cities, it would be proper to refer to elders as plural.[41]

Gerald Cowen sees the singular pastor as fitting within the scriptural pattern.[42] Still another who sees the singularity of pastors as the most common New Testament model is Manfred Kober.[43] This writing will not attempt to solve the issue, as that would require many pages. It is important to notice that there are examples in the Scripture which give the local church direction, but there are no commands about one or multiple elders. The common accusation that multiple elders will dilute the character of church leadership is simply untrue. So is the notion that the single pastor will corrupt both leadership and the church.[44] Examples of the opposite are legion in our day and have been through the centuries. Charles Spurgeon, for instance had a board of elders, but if there were ever a "one man show" for Sunday worship, it was Charles Spurgeon. Two things need to be mentioned with regard to this question: First, clearly, the larger the congregation, the greater the number of elders/pastors will be necessary. Second, as there are requirements of spiritual maturity for overseers (1 Tim. 3:1-7), no church should have multiple elders unless there are multiple men who possess the gifts and qualifications to do the work of a pastor.

An excellent comment about plurality of elders and congregational government is given by Deckert:

> Regardless of the conclusion to which one comes on the plurality issue, . . . congregational polity must be maintained if NT doctrine and example are to be heeded. It is possible for a church to minister with a plurality of elders and still maintain a congregational form of church government. It is also possible to maintain the congregation's authority under a single pastor. Neither conclusion regarding plurality resolves all questions of polity. Nor does a congregational conclusion regarding polity decide the issue of plurality of elders. Questions regarding both polity and plurality need to be considered and interrelated on a biblical basis.[45]

A question associated with the subject of multiple elders also needs to be addressed, which is, "Should there be one leader among multiple elders?" The Plymouth Brethren have histori-

Chapter 3: Elders and Their Work 87

cally held to the position that there are to be no distinctions in leadership among a group of elders. *A Biblical Theology of the Church* espouses this same position.[46] Strauch, coming from the Brethren movement, argues, on the contrary, that there is to be leader among the multiple elders.[47] In Jerusalem there were multiple elders, but James was the leader or spokesman for the church (Acts 15:13; 21:18). Paul called the elders of the church in Ephesus to him at Miletus (Acts 20:17ff). Later, Timothy was obviously the leader in this church (1 Tim. 1:3). Paul had many co-workers in his missionary team, but he was doubtless the leader of the group. Therefore, whenever there is a plurality of elders/pastors in a local church, there will be one who will become the main leader. Hans Finzel states, "Leaders should lead, not just implement consensus. When no one is in charge chaos ensues. I firmly believe in the need for a single person to be in charge as opposed to a committee."[48] Some Christians emphatically assert that in their church there is no main leader: "The elders together lead the church." After a certain amount of acquaintance with the church, however, the leadership of one person will be evident.

Gene Getz, who earlier in his ministry minimized the idea of a leader among the elders, changed his perception of the matter after ten years of application of his principles in church work in Dallas.

> If you had asked me ten years ago, "What makes this church work?" I would have said, "Humanly speaking, it's our multiple leadership, primarily the elders." Today, I'd answer that question by saying, "Our elders are key, but I'm the key to helping the elders function." I don't mean to sound egotistical, but I'm more aware of the role I have to play behind the scenes – communicating, motivating, phoning every elder who misses a meeting to fill him in on what happened. My style is the same as before – laid back but working like crazy. The difference is now I'm willing to admit I'm leading. In the early days I overreacted to authoritarian leadership styles – which I still think are unfortunate – but I've always led. Now I feel I'm more honest with myself and others about the importance of a strong leader, particularly in a growing church, and yet also developing a strong multiple leadership that does lead as a team.[49]

Moreover, the existence of an individual leader among multiple elders/pastors does not require that all others are simply "yes men." Group dynamics require a leader for the group. That does not, however, mean the group cannot make decisions together. MacArthur argues that in a group of elders, the only biblical method of decision-making is by consensus.[50] Getz counters this idea strongly:

> When we first started our ministry in Dallas, we had seven or eight elders who met regularly. As a small group, we made decisions by consensus; it was a beautiful experience. . . . As the group became larger (we now have nearly forty elders), we still achieved consensus. But later we found out certain people disagreed but were afraid to express their views and possibly bog everything down. They went along because they didn't want to break up the consensus. Finally some of them spoke up and disagreed . . . Then it dawned on some of us that we really were operating with a sloppy voting system. We were saying to the group, "Does anybody disagree?" We were taking a negative vote, rather than both a negative and a positive vote. What we needed to do was give people the right to say "I agree" or "I disagree," take a vote, and then agree to disagree on certain significant issues.[51]

At this point it is appropriate to deal briefly with the concept of distinctions between elders. John Calvin advanced the idea that elders are to be distinguished from "teaching elders." He drew this concept from 1 Timothy 5:17:

> We may learn from this, that there were at that time two kinds of elders; for all were not ordained to teach. The words plainly mean that there were some who "ruled well" and honorably, but who did not hold the office of teachers. And, indeed, there were chosen from among the people men of worth and of good character, who, united with the pastors in a common council and authority, administered the discipline of the Church, and were a kind of censors for the correction or morals.[52]

But this distinction is not what the text states. It simply says that some elders were especially (*malista*) laboring in teaching the Word. In fact, Paul affirmed that all elders must possess the ability to teach the congregation (1 Tim. 3:2 – *didaktikos*).[53] He could not have devised the opposite teaching two chapters later.

Not only must all elders be able to teach, the New Testament teaches that all elders must be able to shepherd: "I exhort the elders among you . . . shepherd the flock of God among you" (1 Pet. 5:1-2; see also Acts 20:28). *malista* "is not intended to indicate a different office, but to distinguish from others those who assiduously apply themselves to the most important, as well as the most difficult, part of their office, public teaching."[54] When one holds the concept that not all elders need the gift of teaching, then quite naturally, one will interpret the 1 Timothy 5 text as Calvin did.

Is the Election of Pastors/Elders by the Congregation a Biblical Procedure?

Most free churches (as well as many Lutheran churches) are convinced that the testimony of Scripture makes it clear that the elders (pastors) of a church are to be chosen by the church as a whole. Two passages deal directly with the choosing of elders for local churches. Titus 1:5 states that Titus is to be responsible for authorizing (*kathistemi*)[55] elders in every city. Acts 14:23 states that at the end of the missionary trip of Paul and Barnabas elders were appointed in every church. The logical antecedent of "choose" or "appoint" (*cheirotoneo*)[56] is Paul and Barnabas.

There are, essentially, two positions on the interpretation of this passage. The first is that Paul and Barnabas did the entire act alone.[57] The second position is that the selection was done by the congregations and approved by the apostles.[58] Knight, representing the latter view, equates the appointing with the laying on of hands by the apostles in Acts 6, and argues,

> It would appear that both Paul, addressing Titus, and Luke in Acts 14 are compressing what takes place by speaking only of the last act, i.e., appointment or laying on of hands, and do not feel it necessary to relate the steps that lead up to that act (which are related in Acts 6).[59]

To use these passages for present day choice of elders/overseers, one must first observe that neither Paul, Barnabas, nor Titus are ever called "elders." Strauch correctly points out that there is no New Testament passage which directly demonstrates that elders appointed elders.[60] So Acts 14:23 and Titus 1:5 are, in themselves, not directives for all time about the process of choosing elders. Much of the disagreement about how to apply these passages is based on a faulty interpretation of the roles of Paul, Barnabas, and Titus in the book of Acts and the Pastoral Epistles. They were not elders, but missionaries. In any new church planting work, it is crucial that one or more experienced missionaries assist or even guide in the selection of new pastors. To do otherwise is to invite disaster. The newly formed congregation, in fact, normally looks to a missionary for such a guiding hand.[61]

To understand how mature congregations are to choose pastors/elders, one must look to the analogy of other church government decisions in the New Testament. Kistenmacher notes,

> By following the analogical rule of comparing Scripture with Scripture, we learn that in Acts Luke presents "three typical pictures of election and ordination in the cases of Matthias (1:23-26), the Seven (6:1-6), and Paul and Barnabas (13:1-3)." These analogies demonstrate that the assemblies chose the candidates, then prayed and fasted, and afterward ordained them. Likewise, in the case of the elders in Lyconia and Pisidia, the apostles approved the selections made by the churches and, after prayer and fasting, appointed them.[62]

Ridderbos' comments on this matter are very perceptive:

> At first sight it may appear that all sorts of ideas run through each other here and that on this ground one could now defend apostolic succession, then again direct calling by the Spirit, in a third instance designation to office by means of prophetic voices, finally also investiture with office as the act of the church only.
>
> When one surveys the whole, however, it is evident that in each investiture with and acceptance of official power to act and authority two different elements are present: first, Christ himself, who will not only have the office established and maintained in the way of the transference of power once given, but works in the church through his Spirit, so that the work of

the Lord on earth may be done, his church be built up, and his power to act invested in persons qualified to that end. Second, the church itself, which designates and chooses these persons and in the name of the Lord enables them to enter upon the work charged to them.[63]

Calvin argues that this type of activity, where leaders oversee elections, was common in deliberative assemblies in the Roman world. With respect to Acts 14:23 and other passages, he states,

> Therefore they selected two; but the whole body, as was the custom of the Greeks in elections, declared by a show of hands which of the two they wished to have. Thus, it is not uncommon for Roman historians to say, that the consul who held the *comitia* elected the new magistrates, for no other reason but because they received the suffrages, and presided over the people at the election. . . . We must interpret the above passages, so as not to infringe on the common right and liberty of the Church.[64]

To some extent, the Bible leaves the process open. The pattern of the whole congregation being involved in selection of officers is plain in the New Testament. So is the pattern of established preachers participating, as a distinctive group, in the process of selection of new pastors/elders.

Some would argue that letting a church choose its pastor is equivalent to the absurd notion of having a flock of sheep choose its shepherd.[65] The argument is an old one, as is clear from the writings of the reformers. Turretin responds that the protest is correct for irrational sheep, but not for rational sheep. "As they distinguish the voice of the shepherd from that of a hireling and of the wolf, so they know how to elect suitable pastors."[66] Luther argues the same way in his tract asserting the Scriptural mode of congregational choice, citing such passages as Matthew 7:15ff; 1 Thessalonians 5:21; 2 Thessalonians 2:1-3; and Matthew 24:4-5.[67] For Luther, the ability of believers to understand Scripture and their ability to choose the right preacher went hand in hand. Like all analogies, that of pastor/shepherd: congregation/sheep cannot be pressed in all its details. Pastors may be called upon to sacrifice their lives for their congregation, but they cannot, like the Good Shepherd, die for the sins of the sheep. Though in one sense, elders are shepherds, in another sense, they are also feeble sheep.

Turretin presents a long discussion on the election of the pastor by the congregation. Among other arguments, he makes the following:

> The authority and right of action belongs to the superior, not to the inferior. Now the church is superior to pastors, not pastors to the church; the church does not belong to the pastors, but the pastors to the church. "All things are yours," says Paul, "whether Paul, or Apollos, or Cephas" (1 Cor. 3:21-22). Here he rebukes those who gloried in men as heads and for whose sake they raised dissentions and parties among the Corinthians. He shows that they acted falsely because the church is greater than and superior to all. Hence pastors are called servants and ministers of the church: "We are your servants for Jesus' sake" (2 Cor. 4:5). If ministers to the church, they ought to be elected and called by her.[68]

Turretin buttresses his arguments with a listing of quotes by church Fathers who explicitly state that either bishops or elders were to be elected by congregational vote. These witnesses include Tertullian, Origin, Cyprian, Crysostom, Gratian, Ambrose, Theodoret, and Augustine.[69] The teaching of the Didache (15:1)[70] can be added to these. Gibbon points out that as the Christian Church became the imperial Roman Church the Roman emperors had no choice but to accept the church's long tradition of electing bishops by popular sufferage.[71]

As mentioned in Chapter One, Clement of Rome stated in his letter to the Corinthians that the elders in the church in Corinth were appointed by the apostles, "with the consent of the whole church."[72] Clement wrote ca. AD 95. According to tradition, the apostle John was still living. In any case, some people in the Corinthian church who knew the apostle Paul would have been living. Clement could not have misled them. Irenaeus, writing in AD 175 says that Clement had known Paul and Peter personally and conveyed in his letter what they had taught him.[73] These witnesses are not determinative for church doctrine. They do, however, show that the idea of the congregation voting for the pastor is not originally American, or Puritan, or Congregational.[74] It is an ancient prescribed form, going back to the time just after the apostles (if the New Testament is excluded from consideration). Schaff relates that with the beginning of the middle ages,

> . . . the republican element in the election of bishops entirely disappeared. The Greek Church after the eighth century vested the franchise exclusively in the bishops. The Latin Church, after the eleventh century, vested it in the clergy of the cathedral church, without allowing any participation to the people."[75]

The process by which churches choose their elders is widely misrepresented, as though it were the same as a political event or popularity contest. On the contrary, the initial screening is typically done by a search committee, a group of elders, a pastoral staff, or a single pastor. The candidate (or candidates) is then set before the church body for its choice. Bob Whitney, who for many years served in an elder-led church (as distinguished from a congregational one) describes elder selection in the following way: first, the elders choose candidates, who are announced to the congregation. This is followed by a period of days for questioning privately by church members. At a later date, a final list is presented to and affirmed by the congregation.[76] This procedure actually is one of several that fit well within the concept of a congregational model.[77]

Bishops, in the New Testament Sense, Are Local, Not Regional in Their Jurisdiction

Many denominations hold to a three- or even four-tiered ministry in the church. In fact, most professing Christians belong to a church in which the bishop functions as a regional, or "monarchial" authority. That is, the bishop governs many churches within a territory. The pastors submit to him as well.[78] The arguments for this position will be stated, and then answered.

1. The Terms Episkopos *And* Presbyteros *Refer To Two Separate Offices*[79]

The arguments for this position are based on the variety of terms used in the New Testament,[80] or in later documents, such as the *Didache* and *Hermas*.[81] Some, such as Lowndes, base the distinction on such Scriptures like 1 Timothy 5:19-20, the rebuking of an elder. "This, of course, refers to a formal trial by one in authority of persons inferior to him in rank."[82] Another argument for this position is based not on the New Testament, but on the writings of Ignatius.[83] The Roman Catholic Church uses the Statements of Ignatius as much as any Scripture to substantiate their view of the authority of the bishops.[84] "You must all follow the bishop, as Jesus Christ followed the Father, and follow the presbytery as you would the apostles."[85] A third position is to say that it cannot be determined in the New Testament whether the bishop was distinct from the presbyter. This then allows for legitimate development of three offices.[86]

It has been sufficiently established in the beginning of this chapter that the New Testament uses the two terms of this office synonymously.[87] Dunn admits that his evidence for the distinction from the New Testament is scant.[88] The Catholic theologian, Jan Ambaum, affirms that the separate office of priest is not to be found in the New Testament.[89] To this it may be added that the terms "bishop" and "presbyter," as used in the New Testament, applied only to local offices.[90]

The first historical mention of a bishop as distinct from presbyters is found in the writings of Ignatius (AD 110), ten to fifteen years after the death of the last apostle. But the differentiation he made between the two was something new. Note what Streeter says:

> Six of the seven letters are filled with exaggerated and passionate exaltation of the authority and importance of the bishop's office. What nobody questions, nobody defends; over-enthusiastic defense implies the existence of strong opposition. The principle which Ignatius is so concerned to uphold is evidently one by no means universally recognized. . . . The language and tone of Ignatius on the subject of the episcopate is that of a man who had become Bishop of Antioch at a time

when the monarchial status and authority of that office was as yet not sufficiently ancient to be secure. He is fighting a battle which is not yet won.[91]

To establish his teaching about the authority of the bishop, Ignatius never argues from the position of James, or the apostles, or from Timothy and Titus. Instead, as Friend points out,

> His assertion of monepiscopacy as the sole form of church government had nothing to do with 'tradition' or apostolic succession. It was the product of a mystical theology in which he identified his office with that of Christ's high priestly role. The common ground between his concept of episcopacy and that of his contemporaries in Asia was the Eucharist.[92]

Schöllgen has pointed out that Ignatius' view of the bishop cannot be called "monarchial" in the true sense of the word, and that he never demands the subordination of the presbyters to the bishop.[93] Nevertheless, there is a significant difference between the teaching of Ignatius about church leadership and that, which is written by Paul. Notice, for instance, the following statement by Ignatius: "Let everyone respect the deacons as Jesus Christ, just as they should respect the bishop, who is a model of the Father, and the presbyters as God's council and as the band of the apostles. Without these no group can be called a church" (*Ignatius to the Trallians*, 3.1). Erickson argues, that "If we maintain that this trend was not already present within the body of Christ in the New Testament days, we are making the rather large assumption that the church very quickly departed from its New Testament foundations."[94] But the tendency of churches to slide into error is regularly addressed in nearly all of Paul's letters. Before his death the apostle John recorded several departures from New Testament found in contemporary churches (Rev. 2-3). And when one compares the teachings of the New Testament on the subject of church leadership with the assertions of Ignatius, the assumption that there was a quick departure from New Testament foundations isn't very large at all.

2. The Apostles Had Authority Over Many Churches, Thus The Bishops Have Authority Over Many Churches.[95]

Various passages are used to substantiate this claim, including the instructions of Paul to Timothy to instruct and correct in the church at Ephesus (1 Tim. 1-3), and his instruction to Titus to set things in order and appoint elders in every church (Titus 1:3-7). In fact, the apostles were never authorities over particular designated areas. Peter was in Jerusalem, Judea, Antioch (Gal. 2), perhaps Corinth (note the party of Peter in 1 Cor. 3), and likely Rome (1 Pet. 5:13). His teachings were given with authority in the Roman provinces of Asia Minor, where Paul had planted the churches. The words of James and the church of Jerusalem were likewise taken with authority in the churches planted by Paul (Acts 16:4). The writings of Paul were taken as Scripture where they were read (2 Pet. 3:15-16). John originally ministered in Jerusalem (Acts 3-10). From his later writings, it is clear that he ministered in Asia Minor (Rev. 1-3). The book of Acts depicts the other apostles ministering in Jerusalem, but does not relate anything specific about their later labors (though Eusebius 250 years afterward gives extensive history). One can assume that the apostles presided over the existing churches in some way, but there is no indication in the New Testament that they did anything of the kind (outside of their leading the Jerusalem church in Acts 1-8).

When apostles or their representatives visited churches their authority was generally acknowledged (e.g. Acts 8:14ff; 10:36ff). But the limits of apostolic authority are seen in that Paul was sometimes rebuffed as a teacher by some Christians (2 Cor.10: Phil.1:14-17). The shepherding authority of Paul and that of Peter were overlapping and hardly absolute. One can say that the writings of the apostles were taken with authority in the new churches. It is difficult, however, to use the New Testament to define apostolic authority over churches in the sense of a regular watch, care, instruction, and decision-making. Christ indeed promised that the twelve apostles would sit on twelve thrones. That, however, was a promise for their future relation with the twelve tribes of Israel in the Kingdom age (Mt. 19:28; Luke 22:30). The church of the New Testament was a persecuted church. Its apostles did not rule over territories. Instead, after Acts 10 they were regularly on the move (see also 1 Cor. 9:5).

With regard to Paul's instructions to Timothy and Titus, they need to be understood in the light of mission work. Paul, Timothy and Titus were missionaries. Fung calls them "temporary delegates sent to deal with specific situations."[96] Until the churches had indigenous leadership, their work was incomplete. One often finds Paul returning to the works he had begun, in order to correct, instruct and encourage. One has to look long, however, for any description of a hierarchy in the episcopal sense in any of his labors. Ridderbos notes,

> Every trace of an incipient hierarchical order or "apostolic succession" is lacking here. Nor can the *episkopos* to be appointed by them be interpreted as a *primus inter pares,* who would then represent the incipient hierarchy. However clearer in these epistles than in the older ones are the contours with which the ordering of the church is marked, no fundamental shifting is to be found here that would justify the qualification of (transition to) "early catholicism," or which would consist in the transition from the liberty of the Spirit to a principle of tradition and legitimacy.[97]

If regional bishops are proposed, then there must, of necessity, be a regional church. This is the direct teaching of the Catholic Church:

> Apart from missionary territory, the world is divided up into dioceses, and in each diocese the bishop has the power to govern. He is the head of it; he has the responsibility of seeing that the laws of the Church are kept and that no abuses creep in.[98]

Radmacher also points out that

> All the leading Reformers, who heroically freed the church from the Roman Catholic Church and pope, fastened a state church upon the people wherever they went and that the churches that stood for absolute religious liberty were persecuted by these state churches.[99]

One can speak of "the Church in America" and most of those listening would understand what is meant. However, this is not in any sense biblical terminology. Bauer lists four meanings for the word *ekklesia* in the New Testament: 1) an assembly, 2) a gathering or meeting, 3) the congregation of the Israelites, 4) the Christian church. The fourth category includes the church or congregation in one place, house churches, and the church universal.[100] O'Brien states,

> Although we often speak of a group of congregations collectively as "the church" (i.e., of a denomination), it is doubtful whether Paul (or the rest of the NT) uses *ekklesia* in this collective way. Also, the notion of a unified provincial or national church appears to have been foreign to Paul's thinking.[101]

Of special interest for this point is Acts 9:31: "So the church throughout all Judea and Galilee and Samaria enjoyed peace." This verse is best understood as *ekklesia* in an extended sense. "Church," here means any of, or all of the churches in the areas. Three regions are mentioned, not one. There is no indication of an organization of these churches. Instead, the spiritual unity of the churches is what is emphasized. This emphasis was important, since the unity between Judaean and Samaritan Christians was not automatic. In 1 Corinthians 15:9 and Galatians 1:13, where Paul mentions his persecution of the *ekklesia* that took place before his conversion, he uses the singular. But in this case, no region is mentioned. When the New Testament speaks of the *ekklesia* in a region, it uses the plural *ekklesiai* (Acts 15:41; Ro. 16:4; 1 Cor. 16:1; 2 Cor. 8:1; Col 1:2,22; Col. 4:16; 1 Th. 1:1; 2 Th. 1:1; Rev.1:4). Acts 9:31 is the one exception to this rule.

Giles argues that there is a discrepancy in the witnesses to the text of Acts 9:31, namely, that some texts have *ekklesia* and the verb following in the singular, while others have both in the plural.[102] He contends that commentaries need to make more of this point before drawing conclusions, and feels that while *ekklesia* should be plural, the verb should be in the plural. O'Brien comments on this passage,

> In one or two NT instances *ekklesia* is found as an extension of the literal, descriptive use of "an assembly" to designate the persons who compose that gathering, whether they are assembled or not. This is a natural extension or linguistic development of group words (note our use of the word "team"), and may explain references such as Acts 8:3; 9:31; 20:17.[103]

Giles takes *ekklesia* in 9:31 as referring to the Jerusalem Church, which had been scattered because of persecution throughout Judaea, Galilee and Samaria.[104]

3. The Bishops Are Successors Of The Apostles.

In the Roman Catholic and the Anglican view, the bishops are the successors of the apostles.[105] The first to assert that bishops became successors of the apostles, and thus had a regional authority, was Theodoret (393-466). Lightfoot responds to this position in the following way:

> For the opinion hazarded by Theodoret and adopted by many later writers, that the same officers in the Church who were first called apostles came afterwards to be designated bishops, is baseless. If the two offices had been identical, the substitution of the one name for the other would have required some explanation. But in fact the functions of the Apostle and the bishop differed widely. The Apostle, like the prophet or the evangelist, held no local office. He was essentially, as his name denotes, a missionary, moving about from place to place, founding and confirming new brotherhoods.[106]

Lightfoot later points out that the episcopate must have been an elevation from the presbytery, rather than successors to the apostles.[107]

Accompanying this doctrine is the interpretation that Christ gave his commission to the apostles, not to all disciples. This is then handed on successively by the bishops.[108] The change from a missionary church to a hierarchical church was not just a matter of Christians letting professionals do the work. It was a thoroughly formed doctrine that taught the congregation they were incapable of communicating the Word of God to others. That this cannot be true is evident from a simple reading of the New Testament passages on mission work. Jesus commanded the healed demoniac of Gerasa to tell his relatives what great things God had done for him (Luke 8:39). On the day of Pentecost, 120 were baptized in the Holy Spirit (and received the accompanying power to be witnesses – Acts 1:8), and proclaimed the mighty acts of God (Acts 2:1-11). During the persecution after the death of Stephen, "those who had been scattered went about preaching the word" (*euangelizomenoi*—Acts 8:4). This group did not include the apostles (8:2). Parts of this same group went as far as Phoenicia and Antioch, "speaking the word" (*lalountes ton logon*—11:19) and "preaching (*euangelizomenoi*) the Lord Jesus." Later, in Acts 15:3 and 21:3 Luke reports of groups of believers in Phoenicia (and no doubt churches). In Acts 11:21 Luke states that, "a large number who believed turned to the Lord." The interpretation that the commission to evangelize was given to the apostles, who in turn gave it on to the bishops, cannot be defended throughout the book of Acts.

The Roman Catholic, as well as the Anglican view of the Bishop's office is that it is sacramental in character,

> The ministry in which Christ's emissaries do and give by God's grace what they cannot do and give by their own powers, is called "sacrament" by the Church's tradition. Indeed, the ministry of the Church is conferred by a special sacrament.[109]

This sacrament is given through the laying on of hands, from bishop to bishop.[110] The bishops thus receive the Holy Spirit endowment for the office through this laying on of hands.[111] Passages used to substantiate this claim are, for instance, 1 Timothy 4:14 and 2 Timothy 1:7. The 1 Timothy 4 passage states, "Do not neglect the spiritual gift within you, which was bestowed upon you through prophetic utterance with the laying on of hands by the presbytery." In this case, the spiritual gift did not come through the laying on of hands. *meta* does not indicate instrumentality, but accompaniment.[112] BAGD defines it as specifying "other accompanying phenomena."[113] The same usage is found in Acts 14:23; 24:18; 27:10; Luke 17:20; etc. Robertson says accompaniment is the most frequent usage of *meta* in the New Testament.[114] In any case, *meta* never takes the meaning of agency. Kent explains the meaning of laying on of hands in the New Testament,

> The laying on of hands was a symbolic practice in the Old Testament for ordaining special officers (Num. 27:18,23), for symbolizing the transfer of guilt from the sinner to the sacrificial animal (Lev. 16:2), and for bestowal of blessing (Gen. 48:14,20). In each case it symbolized the transfer of something. In the New Testament, the symbolism also refers to the com-

munication of some blessing, but the laying on of the hands is always symbolic, not efficacious.[115]

The Work of Pastoring, Considered from the Biblical Perspective

God's work requires leaders. This is a principle one finds repeatedly in the Bible. Israel had Moses and then Joshua as leaders. Later there were judges, and afterward kings to lead the chosen nation. When the kings ceased, God provided other leaders in the persons of Zerubbabel, Ezra, and Nehemiah. During his ministry, John the Baptist had disciples. In Acts 1-5 Peter becomes the spokesman not only for the 12 disciples, but for the whole church. J. Oswald Sanders states, "God and man are constantly searching for leaders in the various branches of Christian enterprise. In the Scriptures, God is frequently represented as searching for a man of a certain type. Not men, but a man. Not a group, but an individual."[116]

The book of Hebrews tells Christians, "Remember those who led you, who spoke the word of God to you . . . imitate their life" (13:7). Church leaders lead foremost through their example and their teaching. Paul also emphasized the importance of the pastoral example in 1 Timothy 4. Likewise Peter tells elders to use the method of example in their leadership, rather than making demonstrations of authority (1 Pet. 5:3). MacArthur wisely advises, "If you try to lead people without setting a pattern they can follow, they will resist your leadership."[117] Looking at the principle from another direction, Charles Wagner says, "If he (the pastor) is compelled to remind his boards that he is the leader, he is a failure . . . It would be ridiculous for the shepherd to keep repeating, 'I am your shepherd' as he leads his sheep."[118] How to lead by example is not necessarily a question of experience, though that is involved. Rather, leading by example requires that the leader know where the church is supposed to be headed. He also possesses the inner conviction to live like the Bible teaches, and acts on that conviction.

The author of Hebrews goes on to say, "Obey your leaders, and submit to them; for they keep watch over your souls, as those who will give an account" (13:17). A pastor is responsible not only for his own spiritual well being but also for that of every member. For this reason he is to be respected by all the members. His teaching is to be heeded. Hebrews 13:17 goes so far as to emphasize both an inward (*peithesthei* —"be persuaded, be convinced")[119] and an outward (*hypekete*) submission to the teaching of church leaders. The admonition is thus rather thorough. Paul states, "But we request of you, brethren, that you know those who diligently labor among you, and have charge over you in the Lord and give you instruction."[120] The word here translated "know" (*eidenai* — aorist infinitive of *oida*) means in this context "to respect."[121] This is Paul's consistent teaching to churches about the attitude the members were to have towards their leaders.[122]

The work of a preacher (including elders) requires a call from God (1 Tim. 4:14; 2 Tim.1:6). Paul declares, "Let a man so account of us as of the ministers of Christ, and stewards of the mysteries of God" (1 Cor. 4:1). Later in Titus 1:7 he calls the overseer of a church "God's steward." The word for "steward," in both cases, *oikonomos*, used both among secular Greek writers, in rabbinical literature, and the LXX for a person officially in charge of managing the property of someone else.[123] Spurgeon states,

> Surely the steward must hold the office from the Master. He cannot be a steward merely because he chooses to be so, or is so regarded by others. If any of us should elect ourselves stewards to the Marquis of Westminster, and proceed to deal with his property, we should have our mistake very speedily pointed out to us in the most convincing manner.[124]

This does not negate a personal desire to become an elder, for 1 Timothy 3:1 declares that the desire to become an overseer is a proper one. But more than desire and gifts are required for the office. The candidate needs to be certain of God's calling as well.

The ministry of pastor will also require suffering (2 Tim. 2:3) and hard work (2 Tim. 2:6). Referring to the spirit pervading modern western culture, McLachlan states,

There is no doubt that serving others is out; serving self is in. Even within the realm of ministry, the model for Christian service has become that of a corporation executive rather than that of a humble servant. The CEO syndrome has invaded the New Testament church. While management models from the business world may help us in becoming *efficient* at what we do in the ministry, it's only a whole-hearted embracing of the servant's model of Jesus Christ that will enable us to become *effective* at what we do in the ministry. Efficient managers master routines, but effective leaders impact lives.[125]

Strauch describes the work of the pastor well when he says,

Based on Paul's example and the evidence of Scripture, we see that true elders do not dictate, but direct. They do not command the consciences of their brethren, but appeal to their brethren to faithfully follow God's Word. They suffer and bear the brunt of difficult people and problems so the lambs are not bruised. They bear the misunderstandings and sins of others so the assembly may live in peace. They lose sleep so others may rest.[126]

A pastor/elder needs to be a teacher. Following the pattern of Paul, he needs to teach "the whole counsel of God." That means he is to preach from all of God's Word, not just those portions or books that he or his audience favors. Couch makes the following observation from the analogy of literal shepherds and sheep:

Shepherds should pick the right pastures. The sheep eat the grass the shepherd leads them to. If the sheep stop to munch something they should not, with a long stick the shepherd will "spook" them to move on. He is responsible for their feeding. Some pastors today are giving the sheep what they want, not what they need.[127]

Paul emphasized in other places the importance of preaching and teaching God's Word (e.g. 1 Tim. 4:12-16). His strongest final admonition to Timothy was to "preach the Word" (2 Tim. 4:1-2).

Pastors need to watch over the flock. Getz notes,

There is nothing that is not included in this task. It involves total and complete oversight of the family or the church. Put another way, God holds the father responsible for the overall leadership in a home, and He holds the elders responsible for the overall leadership in a church.[128]

One of the primary tasks of the pastor is to guard the congregation from false teaching (Acts 20:29; Tit. 1:5-9). False teachers were and are a major and frequent problem for churches. The literature, seminars, videos, radio and television programs and workshops of false teachers are accessible everywhere. Their methods are subtle. Their followings are huge. Their coffers are full. They mention Christ but do not know him. [129] The danger they present to Christian churches is not new. False teachers were predicted by Paul (1 Tim. 4; 2 Tim. 3), Peter (2 Pet. 2), and Jude. In AD 150 Justin Martyr related that false teachers who presented themselves as Christians were wide spread in the Roman world.[130] One does not need to look beyond man's corrupt nature or the reality of the devil to find the cause of false teachers in our day.

False teachers and their followers do active personal work. From time to time they show up in Bible believing local churches. It is the pastor's responsibility to wisely and boldly protect his people, without making the topic of false doctrine his hobbyhorse. Strauch comments on the problem and the ministry,

> It is not easy to be watchful! The Old Testament proves that, for Israel fell into false religion time and again. The natural human tendency is to become less alert, to become weary, unconcerned, and selfish. Alertness takes considerable time, thinking, energy, and work. It isn't easy to answer questions, speak to changing issues, answer criticism, stand against other people, and confront false teachers. At times vigilance is wearisome. But it must be done![131]

The most likely spiritual wolf to enter the local congregation is not a famous theologian whose interviews and heresies make the pages of national news magazines. Spiritual wolves typically lie much closer and are therefore even more dangerous. They usually get their start in the church, not outside of it. Paul warned, "and from among your own selves men will arise, speaking perverse things, to draw away the disciples after them." (Acts 20:30). Philip Ryken makes the following observation,

Chapter 3: Elders and Their Work 105

Doctrinal error that leads a church astray almost never arises from the laity, but nearly always comes from the clergy. One of the most likely places for heresy to originate is from the church pulpit or the seminary lectern.[132]

The responsibility for the successes of apostasy in Christendom throughout church history can primarily be laid at the feet of pastors who did not take Paul's admonition seriously to take care of their own hearts and to watch out for wolves in sheep's clothing.

Shepherding the flock requires the attention of pastors. They need to be well aware of what is going on in the lives of their people. Christians get into sin for various reasons. Some get very discouraged trying to live the Christian life. Others encounter serious family or psychological problems. Still others have debilitating illnesses. Pastors dare not neglect these people. Sometimes the criticisms troubled Christians send the way of the pastor or the church are simply a method of letting off steam because of difficulties in their lives. The quicker the pastor attends to the problems of troubled members, the smaller the effects of the problems will be. Jesus took time for the poor, the downtrodden, the sick, and the discouraged. They didn't look and smell any more beautiful to him than they do to us. If the pastor/elder will follow his example, he will understand Christ better (and will become a better preacher, too).

Pastors need to develop leadership in the church (2 Tim. 2:1-2). This is an important, but often forgotten responsibility. John C. Maxwell argues that whether in a church or a secular organization, leaders who develop other leaders create a large advantage for their organization over those who do not: "Leaders who develop followers grow their organization only one person at a time. But leaders who develop leaders multiply their growth, because for every leader they develop, they also receive all of that leader's followers."[133] He also argues that it is the most effective way of providing a continuum in the church after a pastor leaves.[134]

Getz adds a word of warning,

> One of the most tragic things happening in our culture today is that highly gifted men are attempting to train ordinary men to

> be like themselves. Unfortunately, these ordinary men (who make up the majority of us) have neither the capacity nor the ability to become this kind of leader. The result is frustration. Or even more tragic, these men attempt to imitate the life of a multitalented man and end up a total failure – often splitting the church, hurting the body of Christ, and eventually leaving the ministry.[135]

Nevertheless, Getz agrees that the gifted pastor should be active in training other men. As they do, however, they need to think realistically.[136]

If pastors develop leaders within the congregation, they will have to spend personal time with specially chosen people. The work of training leaders will require honesty, sacrifice, love and dedication for those being trained. Sanders says, "The principle thing is to trust them. Blunders are the inevitable price of training leaders."[137]

The pastor/elder functions between two limits: on the one hand is the limit of the Word of God, on the other hand is the will of the congregation. His ministry moves in this structure. There is no place for despotism. The cult leader Jimmy Jones, who led hundreds of his followers to death by suicide, threw his Bible away years before. Finzel calls despotism, when found in the Bible-believing church, "the apostolic style"[138] and says,

> The apostolic style stands at the opposite end of the continuum from the leader who sees his primary role as managing the resources of a team. The apostle views truth as coming down from on high. The apostle knows the battle plan and where the team will go. It is the team's responsibility to implement the dreams and visions which were singularly presented to the leader. That approach may sound spiritual, but I don't believe it is biblical. The age of the apostles – men like Peter and Paul, who really did receive divine inspiration – is over.[139]

It may be that a pastor has found a better method for the ministry of the people of his church. But even if this method is fully biblical, he is not given the authority to force his people to do it. He leads by teaching and example (1 Pet. 5:1-4). With patience, he can usually get his congregation going in a good direction. Jefferson wisely explains,

> It is commonplace that a minister is a leader, and yet not every minister knows how to lead. In other words, he is not a good pastor. Some ministers try to drive. Their fatal weakness is an inability to see that shepherds cannot drive. Such men are always cutting, lashing, forcing, and therefore always getting into trouble. They are continually quarreling with their people, and for no other reason than that they do not know how to lead. They push and do not draw, they shove and do not woo. They believe in propulsion and not in attraction. They lack the magic of the shepherd touch. They do not know human nature, they do not realize that men, like sheep, must be led.[140]

On the other hand, the Bible doesn't allow for any worldly compromise in teaching, in evangelism, in discipline, or in relationships to other churches or organizations. Even when the congregation is longing for compromise, an elder has to reject it (even if it means his removal from his ministry). The decision to listen to the will of the people instead of the voice of God has terrible consequences (1 Sam. 15).

In his discussion of pastoral leadership, Joseph Stowell points to a series of false methods practiced by pastors, such as personal charm, being a dictator, manipulating , playing politics, etc. Following 1 Timothy 4:12 he lays a stress on gaining the respect of the congregation. It is the most crucial point of pastoral leadership.[141] Understanding this principle removes a fair amount of tension pastors feel about getting the people of the church to follow them. Note what Stowell says,

> It is interesting to note that Scripture does not require that we have positive growing relationships with everyone, but it does require that we minister in relationships marked by respect that will enable even those who do not like or appreciate us to follow our shepherding work.[142]

This chapter makes no attempt to describe church structure in the form of a flow chart, or to give details on how to conduct church business. That is not to say that these are not worthwhile. Instead it has been the object of this chapter to explain the position and ministry of the pastor/elder, as seen from a biblical perspective. The pastor or pastors of a church will find that as they improve their performance of ministry, enhance their communication, take their responsibilities more seriously and balance them, grow in their love for their Lord, for his Word, and for his flock, that things will go more smoothly when it is time for a business meeting.

Recommended for Further Study

(Most of the recommended books listed at the end of the previous chapter are also applicable to the concepts of this chapter, as can be observed in the footnotes.)

Spurgeon, Charles. *Lectures to my Students.* (There are various editions of this work. Every English-speaking preacher should own one.)

Jefferson, Charles. *The Minister as Shepherd.* Hong Kong: Christian Literature Crusade, 1973.(A heartwarming, practical, and convicting book on the role of shepherding by a congregational pastor of an earlier generation. It goes right to the core of what shepherding is all about and is an excellent source of advice for modern preachers.)

Strauch, Alexander. *Biblical Eldership*, 2nd ed. Littleton: Lewis and Roth, 1995. (A very good exegetical volume by a Plymouth Brethren teacher, with an emphasis on the local congregation. For Strauch, biblical eldership phased out after the apostles and was revived beginning with George Mueller.)

Cowen, Gerald. *Who Rules the Church?* Nashville: Broadman and Holman, 2003. (95 pages of this book are devoted to the definition of the pastor/elder, the nature of his office and his service. It is an exegetical work. Cowen makes apt contributions on the subjects of a ministerial call and the phrase "husband of one wife.").

Kober, Manfred. *The Case for the Singularity of the Pastor,* Ankeny: Faith Baptist Bible College, n.d. (As the title indicates, this booklet argues that while not mandated the singular Pastor in

Chapter 3: Elders and Their Work 109

the local church is a bona fide scriptural practice. Though brief, it is well argued.)

Kroll, Woodrow. *The Vanishing Ministry*. Grand Rapids: Kregel, 1991.

Macartney, Clarence. *Preaching Without Notes*. Grand Rapids: Baker, 1976. (There is far more in this volume than merely how to preach without notes.)

Bruce, A.B. *The Training of the Twelve*. Grand Rapids: Kregel, 1984. (This book is particularly helpful in understanding the work of leadership development. Bruce explains how with purpose, patience and precision Jesus trained his disciples.)

Maxwell, John C. *The 21 Irrefutable Laws of Leadership*. Nashville: Thomas Nelson, 1998. (This insightful book boils leadership down to rather simple principles, which the author understands first hand. I distance myself from his practice of replacing all professional pastoral people as a new head-pastor. In the New Testament, continuity of spiritual direction is more a priority than growth.)

Gangel, Kenneth O. *Feeding and Leading*. Grand Rapids: Baker, 1996. (Gangel's book is mentioned again here particularly on account of its helpful chapter on Leadership Development, "Training for Godliness and Competence.")

McLachlan, Douglas. *Reclaiming Authentic Fundamentalism*. Independence: American Association of Christian Schools, 1991. (An appeal to ministers from the historic protestant fundamentalist background to pursue an authentic Christian ministry. This book will also benefit those ministers of Christ who do not call themselves fundamentalists.)

Sangster, W.E. *The Craft of the Sermon*. Philadelphia: Westmnister, 1961. (A challenging book on the subject by the late bishop of the English Methodist Church. Sangster understood how to interact with God and with a sinful, needy world in his sermon preparation.)

MacArthur, John. *The Master's Plan for the Church*. Chicago: Moody, 1991.

Turretin, Francois, *Institutes of Elenctic Theology*, Vol. III. James T. Dennison, Jr, ed. Phillipsburg: Presbyterian and Reformed, 1997. (Particularly chs. XVI – XXVIII.)

Hughes, R. Kent and Bryan Chapell. *1&2 Timothy and Titus*. (Preaching the Word series) Wheaton: Crossway Books, 2000. (An outstanding all-around commentary on these NT books for the average English-speaking pastor. The authors combine scholarship, spiritual teaching, application, and practical wisdom in their exposition).

Kent, Homer A., Jr. *The Pastoral Epistles*. Chicago: Moody, 1958.

Knight, George W. III. *The Pastoral Epistles* (NIGTC). Grand Rapids: Eerdmans, 1992.

Notes

[1] Two other designations, οἱ ἡγούμενοι, participial form of ἡγέομαι) in Hebrews 13:7, 17 and οἱ προιστάμενοι, are also used of church leaders who function in the teaching, guiding capacity. But as they are participles, they do not appear to have been used as titles for the office of elder. Nevertheless, the passages containing them will be mentioned as well.

[2] John Calvin, *Institutes of the Christian Religion*, Vol. II, Henry Beveridge, Trans. (Grand Rapids: Eerdmans, 1972 rprn.), 321 (IV.III.8). The *Confessio Fidei Galliciana*, also prepared by Calvin (1559), appears to distinguish between pastors and overseers. See Philip Schaff, ed. *The Creeds of Christendom*, Vol.III (Grand Rapids: Baker, 1990 rprn.), 376-378. One modern theologian of the congregational persuasion who distinguishes the offices of pastor or teacher, elder, and deacon is Ed Glasscock. See his article, "The Biblical Concept of Elder," *BibSac*144.573 (Jan-Mar, 1987), 76. In a similar way, "Presbyterianism operates with a three-fold ministry of preacher, elder, and deacon. It may be difficult to fit this into the NT nomenclature but it harmonizes well with the basic contours of apostolic polity." D. MacLeod, "Church Government," *New Dictionary of Theology*, Sinclair B. Ferguson and David F. Wright, eds. (Downers Grove: InterVarsity, 1988), 145.

[3] Rolland McCune makes the following clarification on the relationship between gifts and offices: "Gifts are special endowments bestowed sovereignly by God either providentially or miraculously. The local church cannot grant or confer such gifts; it may only recognize them and use them within its ministry. See 1 Cor. 12:4-11. Gifts carry no ecclesiastical authority within the local church." Rolland McCune, "Systematic

Theology III" (Seminary Notes. Allen Park: Detroit Baptist Seminary, n.d.) 103. Robert Cook's analysis is more extensive: "Gifts are bestowed by God (1 Cor. 12:11); offices are conferred by the local church (6:5). Gifts are sovereignly given to all believers (1 Cor. 12:11); offices are to be filled according to specified standards (1 Tim. 3:1-13). Gifts are related to general ministry and the Body at large (Eph. 4:7-16) as well as to the local assembly (1 Cor. 12:27-28), while offices relate to specific ministry and to the local church, only (cf. 1 Tim. 3:5). One need not hold office to possess or exercise a gift, but one should not hold office, as biblically described, without possessing qualifying gifts). W. Robert Cook, "Systematic Theology in Outline Form," (Portland: Western Conservative Baptist Seminary, n.d.)165-166. Even for this analysis qualification is necessary. "Office" is not a proper Greek New Testament word for the context of the local church. Saucy goes so far as to say that, "What are often viewed as church 'offices' are in reality church 'services.'" Robert Saucy, "Authority in the Church," in *Walvoord: A Tribute*, Donald K. Campbell, ed. (Chicago: Moody, 1982), 235. Saucy also uses the word "function." Even this borders on being an extra term. It is obvious that in the English language, theologians must adopt terms to describe what is taught on this matter in the New Testament.

[4] Whether the leaders of the Jewish Synagogue were called *presbyteroi* has become a debated subject. Campbell states, "The often repeated statement that the synagogue provided a model for the church in the matter of eldership is seriously misleading. . . . Jewish civic communities referred to their councils as 'elders,' but that hardly provides a model for the leadership of worshipping congregations." R. Alstair Campbell, "The Elders of the Jerusalem Church," *Journal of New Testament Studies*, 44 (1993), 513. Campbell also cites the following in support of this view: A.E. Harvey, "Elders," *JTS* 25 (1974), J.G. Sobosan, "The Role of the Presbyter," *Scottish Journal of Theology*, 27 (1974), and M. Karrer, "Das Urchristliche Ältestenamt," *Novum Testamentum*, 32 (1990), among others.

[5] Bo Reike, "πρέσβυς, κ.τ.λ." *Theological Dictionary of the New Testament*, VI. Geoffrey Bromiley, trans. (Grand Rapids: Eerdmans, 1964), 653.

[6] Ed Glasscock, "The Biblical Concept of Elder," *BibSac* 144.573 (Jan-Mar, 1987), 68. He argues this from the age of Jesus as he began his ministry, the minimal age of the members of the Sanhedrin, and the age at which Levites entered full service. However, Num. 8:24 gives the minimum age for service of the Levites as 25 years.

[7] Ibid., 70.

[8] Robert Browning, "How Democratic was Ancient Athens?" *The Good Idea:Democracy in Ancient Greece*, John A. Koumoulides (New Rochelle: Caratzas, 1995), 61.

[9] David Mappes, "The Elder in the Old and New Testaments," *BibSac* 154.613 (Jan-Mar, 1997), 87.

[10] There are two views about the meaning of the phrase, ποιμένος καὶ διδασκάλους in Eph. 4:11. One is to translate it, "pastors and teachers," thus Paul is talking about five gifts. The other is to translate it "Pastors, who are teachers," thus four gifts, the last two words referring to one person. The following discussion by Wallace on this matter is helpful. "The uniting of these two groups by one article sets them apart from the other gifted leaders. Absolute distinction, then, is probably not in view. In light of the fact that elders and pastors had similar functions in the NT, since elders were to be teachers, the pastors were also to be teachers. Further, presumably not all teachers were elders or pastors. This evidence seems to suggest that the ποιμένας were a part of the διδασκάλους

in Eph. 4:11 . . . Thus Eph. 4:11 seems to affirm that all pastors were to be teachers, though not all teachers were to be pastors. Daniel B. Wallace, *Greek Grammar Beyond the Basics* (Grand Rapids: Zondervan, 1996), 284.

[11] Note his whole discussion of this verse. William L. Lane, *Hebrews 9-13* WBC (Dallas: Word, 1991), 555. ἡγούμενοι is a word that frequently occurs in the LXX of political and military leaders. Dods and Montifore argue that the use of the word in Hebrews is an indication that the organization of the community was not so well developed that it had Elders/Overseers. See Marcus Dods, *The Epistle to the Hebrews* (Expositors Greek Testament, Vol. IV), W. Robertson Nicoll, ed. (Grand Rapids: Eerdmans, 1979 rprn.), 376, and Hugh William Montifore, *The Epistle to the Hebrews* HNTC (Peabody: Hendrickson, 1987 rprn.), 242. This can hardly be the case, however, unless one posits that the Book of Hebrews was written before the events of Acts 11, 14 and 15, where "Elders" are specifically mentioned as leaders of churches (Dods dates Hebrews at AD 63 or later, 13 years after the events of Acts 15). It is more likely that the writer of Hebrews is using the term ἡγούμενοι in a comparative way in the two verses 13:7 and 17. Paul and Silas are called "leading men among the brethren" (Acts 15:22), using this term. They were missionaries but not elders. Most likely the author of Hebrews is emphasizing that the current leaders have the same role and authority, which the first preachers of the church (missionaries) had. Lane also points out that, "Subsequent to Hebrews, the Christian use of the collective term ἡγούμενοι, "leaders,"or the compound προηγούμενοι, "chief leaders," to designate holders of community office appears to be confined to documents associated with the church in Rome." Lane, 526. A further researching of this term would make that which was quite understandable to the readers then more understandable to readers today.

[12] MacArthur, *Elders*, 10.

[13] Hermann W. Beyer, "ἐπίσκοπος" TDNT, II, 610-612.

[14] Ibid., 612.

[15] Ibid.

[16] Ibid., 610.

[17] Ibid., 619.

[18] Hans Küng, *The Church*, Ray and Rosaleen Ockenden, Trans. (Wellwood: Search Press Limited, 1968). 388.

[19] Ibid., 389.

[20] James B. Lightfoot, *Commentary on Philippians* (Grand Rapids: Zondervan, 1976 rprn), 95.

[21] John Calvin, *Institutes of the Christian Religion, II,* Henry Beveridge, trans. (Grand Rapids: Eerdmans, 1977 rprn), 321 (4.III.8).

[22] Johann Albrecht Bengel, *New Testament Word Studies*, Vol. 1, Charlton Lewis and Marvin L. Vincent, trans. (Grand Rapids: Kregel, 1971 rprn.).

[23] "so geht schon daraus hervor, dass ursprünglich beide Namen sich durchaus auf dasselbe Amt bezogen, wie daher auch haufig beide Benennungen als ganz gleichbedeutend miteinander verwechselt werden." August Neander, *Geschichte der Pflanzung und Leitung der christlichen Kirche durch die Apostel*, Vol. 1 (Gota:Perthes, 1890 rprn.), 228.

[24] Beyer, "ἐπίσκοπος" 615-617.

[25] St. Jerome, *Epistle to Evangelus*, 1.

[26] Irenaeus, *Against Heresies* V.XX, Alexander Roberts and James Donaldson, *The Ante-Nicene Fathers*, Vol. 1 (Peabody: Hendrickson Publishers, 1994 rprn.), 547-548.

[27] Daniel Callam calls the view that bishops and elders were originally identical, "implausible." He bases his view on the evidence that ἐπίσκοπος and πρεσβύτερος have no overlapping usage in the LXX, and on the use of the two words in Ignatius. "Bishops and Presbyters in the Apostolic Fathers," *Studia Patristica*, Vol. XXXI, (1997), 108-111. However, Acts 20 puts the two concepts together. It was written prior to the Epistles of Ignatius.

[28] Strauch, 248.

[29] Charles Jefferson, *The Minister as Shepherd* (Hong Kong: Living Books for All, 1973 rprn.), 63.

[30] Wallace distinguishes between "pastor" and "elder." The former, he rightly calls a gift (Eph. 4:12). He goes on, however, to say that one can function as an elder without the gift of pastor. Daniel B. Wallace, "Who Should Run the Church? A Case for the Plurality of Elders." (internet document), http://www.bible.org/docs/soapbox/caseform.htm. (10/ 28/02). The above discussion contradicts his assertion. Wallace likewise holds that not all elders need to possess the gift of teaching, though all must have the ability to teach. He does not, however, explain what the difference between "gift" and "ability" is. Earl Radmacher sees pastors as a special group of elders who have the gift of pastoring (according to Ephesians 4:11), "The Question of Elders," (Portland: Western Baptist Press, 1977). This book sees pastors and elders as identical in every case.

[31] For a thorough, modern exegetical presentation of this position, see John Piper and Wayne Grudem, eds. *Recovering Biblical Manhood and Womanhood: A Response to Evangelical Feminism* (Wheaton: Crossway, 1993; Andreas J. Köstenberger, Thomas R. Schreiner, and H.Scott Baldwin, eds., *Women in the Church* (Grand Rapids: Baker, 1995); Alexander Strauch, *Biblical Eldership* (Littleton, CO: Lewis and Roth, 1995), 51-66; George W. Knight, *The Pastoral Epistles* NICNT (Grand Rapids: Eerdmans, 1992), 138-149. For the view that women may be elders, see Craig S. Keener, *Paul, Women and Wives* (Peabody, MA: Hendrickson, 1992); Alvera Mickelson, ed. *Women, Authority and the Bible* (Downers Grove: InterVarsity, 1986).

[32] Johannes E. Huther, *Critical and Exegetical Handbook to the Epistles of 1&2 Timothy and Titus*, Meyer's Commentary, Maurice J. Evans, trans. (Winona Lake: Alpha, 1979 rprn), 121.

[33] Aristotle, *Politics*, III.iv.1277, T.A. Sinclair, trans. (London, Penguin, 1962), 182.

[34] Strauch, *Biblical Eldership*, 2nd ed., 35-45. Others include Gene Getz, *Sharpening the Focus of the Church* (Chicago: Moody Press, 1974); Jon Zens,"The Major Concepts of Eldership in the New Testament," *Baptist Reformation Review* 7 (Summer, 1978); Mal Couch, et. al. *A Biblical Theology of the Church*, 155-183); Earl Radmacher, *The Question of Elders* (Portland: Western Baptist Press, 1977); Bruce Stabbert, *The Team Concept* (Tacoma: Hegg Brothers, 1982).

[35] MacArthur, *Elders,* 27

[36] Ibid.

[37] Gene Getz, *Sharpening the Focus of the Church* (Chicago: Moody, 1986), 141-146.

[38] Strauch, *Biblical Eldership*, 2nd ed., 39.

[39] See the very helpful discussion of this subject in L. Cohnen, "Bishop, Presbyter, Elder" *New International Dictionary of New Testament Theology*, Vol. I, Colin Brown, ed. (Grand Rapids: Zondervan, 1975), 192-201.

[40] Nutall, *The Weeping Church*, 89-93. His arguments are more extensive than Wagner's. He stresses rather strongly the importance of singular leadership, 63-64 (although he would not rule out the necessity of multiple pastors for churches).

[41] Charles U. Wagner, *Laborers Together* (Schaumburg, IL: Regular Baptist Press, 1988), 16.

[42] Gerald Cowen, *Who Rules The Church?* (Nashville: Broadman and Holman, 2003), 33-53.

[43] Manfred E. Kober, *The Case for the Singularity of Pastors* (Ankeny: Faith Baptist Bible College, n.d.). "While the New Testament appears to allow for the plurality of pastors in each local church, it does not necessitate this.", 4.

[44] Strauch paints a rather bleak picture of single pastoral leadership, as though it inevitably leads to spiritual conflict and corruption. But this is to overlook so many of the churches in history, as well as those currently in the American culture, which thrive spiritually under a single-pastoral set up. Strauch, 2nd ed., 40-43.

[45] Deckert, "Polity and the Elder Issue," 276.

[46] Couch, 171.

[47] Strauch, 2nd ed. 45-48.

[48] Hans Finzel, *The Top Ten Mistakes Leaders Make* (Colorado Springs: Cook Communications, 2000), 91.

[49] "Sharpening the Pastor's Focus: an Interview with Gene Getz" *Leadership* (Summer, 1985), 13-14. In his latest book on the same subject, Getz restates the conclusion here cited. See Gene Getz, *Elders and Leaders* (Chicago: Moody, 2003).

[50] MacArthur, *Elders*, 12. Nuttall feels that the use of a vote in the church, whether among elders or as a whole, has no Scriptural basis: *The Weeping Church*, 43-46.

[51] "A Biblical Style of Leadership: Gene Getz Debates Larry Richards," *Leadership* (Spring, 1981), 72-73.

[52] John Calvin, *Commentaries on the Epistles to Timothy, Titus, and Philemon*, William Pringle, trans. (Grand Rapids: Baker, 1989 rprn), 138-139.

[53] BAGD, 191.

[54] David Mappes, "The New Testament Elder, Overseer, and Pastor," *Bibliotheca Sacra* 154 (Apr, 1997), 174. For a difference among Presbyterians on this point, see George W. Knight, "Two Offices: Two Orders of Elder," *Presbyterion*, 11 (Spring, 1985), 1-12, and Robert Rayburn, "Three Offices, A Reply to George W. Knight," *Presbyterion*, 12 (Fall, 1986), 105-114.

[55] BAGD, 390.

[56] Ibid., 881.

[57] For those holding this position, see BAGD, 881; Lohse, "χειροτονέω" TDNT, IX, 437; F.J. Foakes Jackson and Krisopp Lake, *The Beginnings of Christianity, Part I* (Grand Rapids: Baker, 1965), 168; Strauch, 165-167; Couch, 192-194. BAGD gives the definition "choose by election" for all other uses of the word in Christian literature, including 2 Cor. 8:19. See also the discussion on the subject in Chapter 2. Strauch and

Couch assert that the opposite view from theirs is based primarily on etymology. But that is wide of the mark.

[58] Those holding this position include John Calvin, *Commentary on the Acts of the Apostles*, Vol. II, Henry Beveridge, trans. (Grand Rapids: Baker, 1989 rprn), 27-28; H.A.W. Meyer, *Critical and Exegetical Handbook of the Acts of the Apostles*, Paton J. Gloag, trans. (Winona Lake: Alpha, 1979 rprn.), 275; Henry Alford, *The Greek Testament*, II, (Chicago: Moody Press, 1958 rprn.), 160-161; John Brown, JFB Commentary (Grand Rapids: Eerdmans, 1973 rprn.) III.2, 99; R.C.H. Lenski, *Interpretation of the Acts of the Apostles* (Minneapolis: Augsburg, 1961), 585-586; Richard Longenecker, *The Acts of the Apostles*, EBC (Grand Rapids: Zondervan, 1981), 439. Simon Kistenmacher, *Acts*, NTC (Grand Rapids: Baker, 1990), 525-526.

[59] George W. Knight, *The Pastoral Epistles*, NIGTC (Grand Rapids: Eerdmans, 1992), 288.

[60] Strauch, 278. MacArthur wants to use 1 Tim. 4:14 as a proof. However, this passage speaks of the elders laying their hands on Timothy for missionary service (in the same analogy as Acts 13:2), not to serve as an elder of a local congregation.

[61] Alexander Rattray Hay, who spent many years in mission work before writing about it, says the following, "To any missionary with experience in new fields, where groups of converts and recently formed congregations require to be cared for, the ministry of Timothy in Ephesus of Titus in Crete, and of the others in the various churches which they visited was entirely normal and necessary." *The New Testament order for Church and Missionary* (Audubon: New Testament Missionary Union, 1947), 99. Charles Chaney, a professor of missions, says, ". . . we need to look at 1 & 2 Timothy and Titus through a different lens – as missionary epistles not as pastoral epistles." "The Pastoral Epistles on Care Giving," *Caring for the Harvest Force*, Tom A. Steffen and F. Douglas P. Pennoyer, eds. (Pasadena: William Carey Library, 2001), 34.

[62] Kistenmacher, 525. The author of this book takes the position that this group genuinely became the church at the time they were baptized with the Holy Spirit as recorded in Acts 2.

[63] Ridderbos, 476.

[64] John Calvin, *Institutes of the Christian Religion*, vol. II, Henry Beveridge, trans. (Grand Rapids: Eerdmans, 1972), 325. Calvin does not precisely relate why he thinks two presbyters would be in view in each action in Acts 14. He also argues in this passage from the meaning of χειροτονέω but his position on the meaning of that word in Acts 14:23, which is rejected by this writing, does not detract from his argument from cultural context.

[65] Couch, 192.

[66] Ibid., 232.

[67] Luther, "Das Recht einer christliche Versammlung" 222-223.

[68] Francois Turretin, *Institutes of Elenctic Theology*, III (Phillipsburg, NJ: Presbyterian and Reformed, 1997), James Dennison, Jr. ed. 227-228.

[69] Turretin, 230-231.

[70] Χειροτονήσατε οὖν ἑαυτοίς.

[71] "It was everywhere admitted, as a fundamental maxim of religious policy, that no bishop could be imposed on an orthodox church without the consent of its members. The emperors, as the guardians of the public peace, and as the first citizens of Rome

and Constantinople, might effectually declare their wishes in the choice of ecclesiastical elections, and, while they distributed and resumed the honours of the state and army, they allowed eighteen hundred perpetual magistrates (bishops) to receive their important offices from the free suffrages of the people." Edward Gibbon, *The Deciline and Fall of the Roman Empire*, Vol I (New York: Modern Library, n.d.), 660-661.

[72] Clement, "The Letter of the Romans to the Corinthians," (45.3) Michael Holmes, ed. *The Apostolic Fathers: Greek Texts and English Translations of their Writings* (Grand Rapids: Baker, 1992), 77-79.

[73] Irenaeus, *Against Heresies* III.3.3, ANF, I, 416.

[74] A typical perception that the process of voting for a pastor is a recent idea, is voiced by Norman Nideng, "It is hard to imagine how the evangelical church came to its worship of the democratic process. It takes a lively imagination to find it in the Scripture." "Stop the Voting: You're Wrecking My Church," *Moody Monthly* (March, 1982), 7.

[75] Philip Schaff, *History of the Christian Church*, Vol. III (Grand Rapids: Eerdmans,1974 rprn), 241.

[76] Bob Whitney, "A Proposal for Elder-Led Church Government," (internet document) http://www.ifca.org/Voice/02May-Jun/whitney.htm (12/31/03).

[77] The wisest procedure in congregational choice of its pastor/elder, is to place one candidate before the congregation for each office to be filled. The congregation simply votes "yes" or "no."

[78] Leon Morris, "Church Government," *Evangelical Dictionary of Theology*, Walter Elwell, ed. (Grand Rapids: Baker, 1984), 239.

[79] Representatives of this view include Callam, 107-111. James D.G. Dunn, *Unity and Diversity in the New Testament* (London: SCM Press, 1984), 112-115; Clayton N. Jefford, "Presbyters in the Community of the Didache," *Studia Patristica*, Vol. XXI (1989), 124-128.

[80] Dunn, "Why Are Elders Not Mentioned In 1 Tim. 3?"

[81] Jefford, 124-128.

[82] Arthur Lowndes, "Bishop: Anglican View," *International Standard Bible Encyclopedia*, Vol. I (Grand Rapids: Eerdmans, 1939), 480.

[83] Callum, 107-111.

[84] *Catechism of the Catholic Church* (London: Doubleday, 1995), 258.

[85] J.B. Lightfoot, J.R. Harmer, and Michael Holmes, eds. *The Apostolic Fathers: Greek Texts and English Translations*, (Grand Rapids: Baker, 1992), 189. *To the Smyrneans*, 8.1.

[86] Wilfried Browning, *A Handbook of the Ministry* (London: Mowbray, 1984), 11-12.

[87] Even the Catholic scholar, Jerome D. Quinn, admits that the two terms in the New Testament designate essentially the same person, "Die Ordination in den Pastorbriefen,"*Communio*, 10 (1981), 414.

[88] Dunn, 114. His view is based more on the position that the Pastoral Epistles were composed after Paul, and that there were various distinct church movements during the time of the New Testament, with variations of church government, including Pauline, Pastoral Epistles, Matthaean, Johannean, and that of the author of Hebrews. Other representatives of this view include A.T. Hanson, *The Pastoral Epistles,* NCBC (Grand Rapids: Eerdmans, 1982) and Ernst Käsemann, *Essays on New Testament Themes*, W.J. Montague, trans. (London: SCM, 1964). Carson, Moo and Morris argue thor-

oughly and effectively against the position that 1 & 2 Timothy and Titus were composed after the death of Paul. See D.A. Carson, Douglas Moo and Leon Morris, *An Introduction to the New Testament* (Grand Rapids: Zondervan, 1992), 359-371. Knight also points out that the notion that Paul did not develop church order and established leadersip positions is contradicted by Paul's earliest epistle. Citing 1 Thessalonians 5:12-13 he says, "Thus we see that from his earliest writings Paul is concerned about a simple but definite form of order and authority in the church and about those whom we may rightly designate spiritual leaders." George A.F. Knight, *The Pastoral Epistles*, NIGTC (Grand Rapids: Eerdmans, 1992), 30.

[89] Jan Ambaum, "Die Identität des Priesters," *Communio*, 10 (1981), 421.

[90] Beyer, "ἐπίσκοπος," 615.

[91] B. H. Streeter, *The Primitive Church* (New York: Macmillan, 1929), 169-170.

[92] W.C.H. Friend, *The Rise of Christianity* (New York: Fortress, 1984), 141.

[93] Georg Schöllgen, "Monepiskopat und monarchischer Episkopat" Eine Bemerkung zur Terminologie," *Zeitschrift zum Neuentestamentlischen Wissenschaft*, 77, 1-2 (1986), 146-151.

[94] Millard Erickson, *Christian Theology* (Grand Rapids: Baker, 1985), 1082.

[95] For this position, see Browning, 9-10; or Thomas Schirrmacher, *Ethik*, Vol. I (Neuhausen: Hännsler, 1994), 539. Schirrmacher follows the outline of Ray Sutton, *Captains and Courts* (Philadelphia, 1992). Schirrmacher has since changed his view on church government.

[96] Ronald Y.K. Fung, "Ministry in the New Testament," *The Church in the Bible and the World*, D.A. Carson, ed. (Grand Rapids: Baker, 1987), 167.

[97] Herman Ridderbos, *Paul: An Outline of His Theology*, John Richard De Witt, trans. (Grand Rapids: Eerdmans, 1975), 477.

[98] John Greenwood, *A Handbook of the Catholic Faith* (New York: Doubleday, 1956), 134.

[99] Earl Radmacher, *The Nature of the Church* (Haysville, NC: Schoettel, 1996), 162.

[100] BAGD, 240-241.

[101] Gerald Hawthorne, Ralph P. Martin, Daniel G. Reid, *Dictionary of Paul and His Letters* (Downers Grove: InterVarsity, 1993), s.v. "Church," by P.T. O'Brien, 124.

[102] Witnesses for the singular include P74, A,B,C. Witnesses for the plural include primarily the Majority Text. Metzger comments, "The range and age of the witnesses which read the singular number are superior to those that read the plural. The singular can hardly be a scribal modification in the interest of expressing the idea of the unity of the church, for in that case we should have expected similar modifications in 15:41 and 16:5, where there is no doubt that the plural number ἐκκλησίαι is the original text." Bruce M. Metzger, *A Textual Commentary on the Greek New Testament* (New York: United Bible Societies, 1975), 367.

[103] O'Brien, 124-125.

[104] Giles, 85-86.

[105] *Catechism of the Catholic Church*, 251, "The bishops have by divine institution taken the place of the apostles as pastors of the Church, in such wise that whoever listens to them is listening to Christ and whoever despises them despises Christ and him who sent Christ." 249; Browning, 8. "Apostolic succession is fundamental to the An-

glican communion." John E. Lynch, "Church, Church Polity," *The Encyclopedia of Religion*, Vol. 3, Mircea Eliade, ed. (New York: Macmillan, 1987), 476.

[106] James B. Lightfoot, "The Christian Ministry" in *St Paul's Epistle to the Philippians* (Grand Rapids: Zondervan, 1976 rprn.), 1905-196.

[107] Ibid., 196-198.

[108] *Catechism of the Catholic Church*, 248-249; Joseph Cardinal Ratzinger, "Die kirchliche Lehre vom sacramentum ordinis," *Communio*, 10 (1981), 439.

[109] *Catechism of the Catholic Church*, 252-253.

[110] Browning, 11 (Anglican); Quinn, 417-419 (Catholic).

[111] Quinn, 417.

[112] Homer Kent, Jr., *The Pastoral Epistles* (Chicago: Moody, 1957), 164.

[113] BAGD, 509. For a similar explanation see Nigel Turner, *Grammar of New Testament Greek*, Vol. III, J.H. Moulton, ed. (Edinburgh: T. & T. Clark, 1963), 269.

[114] A.T. Robertson, *A Grammar of the Greek New Testament* (Nashville: Broadman, 1934), 611.

[115] Kent, 164-165. See also the discussion of Lohse, "χείρ," TDNT, IX, 431, "There is no mention of a power of consecration restricted only to certain individuals."

[116] J. Oswald Sanders, *Spiritual Leadership* (Chicago: Moody, 1980), 18.

[117] John MacArthur, *The Master's Plan for the Church* (Chicago: Moody, 1991), 89-90.

[118] Charles U. Wagner, *The Pastor: His Life and Work* (Schaumburg: Regular Baptist Press, 1976), 25.

[119] BAGD 638.

[120] The word translated, "have charge over" is the present participle form of προίστημι, meaning "be at the head of, rule, direct," but also "give aid, care for". Paul uses it to describe how an overseer should rule his own children. He also uses it to speak of elders "who rule well" (1 Tim. 5:17). The noun form of this word is used for Phoebe (Rom. 16:2) "a helper of many."

[121] BAGD, 556.

[122] In this way the church distinguishes itself from the typical conduct experienced in a political democracy, where leaders are frequently criticized or lampooned.

[123] Otto Michel, "οἰκονόμος," TDNT, V, 149.

[124] Charles Spurgeon, *Lectures to my Students* (Grand Rapids: Baker, 1977 rprn.), 21.

[125] Douglas McLachlan, *Reclaiming Authentic Fundamentalism* (Independence, MO: American Association of Christian Schools, 1993), 41. As evidence of the mentality McLachlan is speaking against, it can be noted that George Barna's *Marketing the Church*, in which he plainly calls the local church "a business," has been a best seller among American clergy. *Marketing the Church* (Colorado Springs: NavPress, 1988), 14.

[126] Strauch, (1986), 26.

[127] Couch, 166-167.

[128] Gene Getz, *Sharpening the Focus of the Church* (Chicago: Moody, 1986), 138.

[129] Even the Buddhist Dahlai Lama speaks positively of Jesus Christ, but he regards himself as the incarnation of God.

[130] Justin Martyr, *Dialogue with Trypho* XXXV. ANF, I, 212.

[131] Strauch, 179.
[132] Philip Graham Ryken, *City on a Hill: Reclaiming the Biblical Pattern for the Church in the 21st Century*. (Chicago: Moody, 2003), 107.
[133] John C. Maxwell, *The 21 Irrefutable Laws of Leadership* (Nashville: Nelson, 1998), 208.
[134] Ibid. 215-224.
[135] Getz, *Sharpening the Focus of the Church*, 176.
[136] Ibid.
[137] Sanders, 218.
[138] Finzel, 93.
[139] Ibid.
[140] Jefferson, 49.
[141] Joseph M. Stowell, *Shepherding the Church* (Chicago: Moody, 1997), 102-116.
[142] Ibid., 104-105.

Chapter 4

Deacons and Their Ministry

> But Jesus called them to himself and said to them, "You know that those who are considered rulers over the Gentiles lord it over them, and their great ones exercise authority over them. Yet it shall not be so among you; but whoever desires to become great among you shall be your servant. And whoever of you desires to be first shall be slave of all. For even the Son of Man did not come to be served, but to serve, and to give his life a ransom for many." (Mark 10:42-45 NKJV)

Human beings, because of their inborn pride, have a tendency to desire to rule over their fellow creatures, whether they are redeemed or not. Beyer notes, "The natural man – and especially the Greek – would see no difficulty in answering the question who is greater, the one who serves or the one who is served. It is obviously the latter."[1] Hans Küng points out that,

> Diakonia means an activity which every Greek would recognize at once as being one of self-abasement: waiting at a table, serving food and pouring wine. The distinction between master and servant was nowhere more visually apparent than at meals, where the noble masters would lie at the table in their long robes, while the servants, their clothes girded, had to wait on them.[2]

Even for the Jewish culture, Burge notes, "Religious service as a 'deacon' was uncommon. In Judaism service was exercised through alms, not serving. Hence in the Greek OT *diakonos* refers only to professional court servants. Waiting at tables was considered below the dignity of the Jewish freeman (cf. Luke 7:44-45)."[3]

Jesus taught the opposite form of thinking. The change he brought was radical. He likewise instituted a rule for all leadership among Christians: leadership comes only through service. The greater the position of leadership, the more the acts and attitudes of a servant will be demanded. Christ came to serve. Following his example, Christians are to serve one another.

The Meaning of the Word "Deacon"

It usually comes as a surprise to those studying the matter for the first time that God chose a title for an office of the church, which means "servant." That is the definition of the Greek word, *diakonos*[4] The word has multiple uses in the New Testament: both secular and sacred; Jesus describes himself as a servant, "I have been among you as one who serves" (*ho diakonon,* Lk. 22:27). Paul describes political rulers as *theou diakonos,* ("servants of God" – Ro. 13:2-4). He uses the term for his co-workers and helpers (Eph. 6:21; Col. 1:7). A preacher of the Gospel is a *diakonos* of the New Covenant (1 Cor. 3:5). The whole church, in fact, is a service-organism (Eph. 4:1-16). But the word eventually was used by the church to designate a particular office. Beyer explains,

> . . . in pre-Christian Greek we never find the words ἐπίσκοπος and διάκονος used in the Christian sense, whether individually or in the distinctive Christian relationship. Early Christianity took over words which were predominantly secular in their current usage and which had not yet been given any sharply defined sense. It linked these words with offices which were being fashioned in the community, and thus gave them a new sense which was so firmly welded with the activity thereby denoted that in all languages they have been adopted as loan-words to describe Christian office-bearers.[5]

Being a deacon does not merely signify an office. The ability to minister is a gift from God. Note the point made by Paul, "And since we have gifts that differ according to the grace given to us, let each exercise them accordingly: if prophecy, according to the proportion of his faith; if service (*diakonian*) in his serving." (Ro. 12:6-7a). The Christian who serves as a deacon in the local church needs to be a person especially gifted in serving. He is one who has a sense for where there might be problems or needs in a church, and possesses an ability to know how to help. He does not need regular instruction of how one goes about serving, to carry out his duties.

The Place of the Deacon in the New Testament

The early church, in its beginning, understood that it was responsible for its members.[6] According to Acts 4:4 there were already 5000 men (*ton andron*) in the membership, not including women and children. Among the group were widows. The complaint came from the Greek-speaking Jews, to the Hebrew-speaking Jews, that their widows were being neglected. Kistenmacher explains,

> From the Pentecost account we learn that devout Jews had come from the dispersion to settle in Jerusalem (2:5-11). Many of these devout Jews were elderly people who wanted to spend the rest of their lives in the holy city. Because they had formerly resided elsewhere, their native tongue was Greek, not Aramaic or Hebrew (which was spoken by the Jews in Jerusalem). Many of these people accepted Christ's gospel and became part of the Christian church.[7]

For this great number of people there was a daily ministry for the widows, for which, evidently, the apostles had been responsible up to that time. But in truth they did not have adequate time to attend to this task, as their main responsibilities lay in prayer and teaching the Word of God (6:2-4). The Jerusalem church agreed with the apostles to choose seven men for the task of serving (*chreia* – which may mean "office," though the more likely meaning is "ministry," or "task").[8] The people chose the seven (6:5). The apostles laid their hands on them, to institute them into their office (6:6).[9] Among the Jews of that time there was a group of seven that led the city.[10] There was also a committee of three men responsible for the care of the poor of the city. All of the citizens of the city gave their alms to the committee, which distributed it to the needy.[11] It is possible that either of these orders existing in the Jewish committee formed the background for the creation of a new ministry in the Jerusalem church. As a result of the creation of the new ministry, the murmuring stopped, the needy were taken care of, and many more people turned to faith in Christ (6:7). Historically this ministry persisted in churches in the Roman Empire. In the middle of the 4th century the church in Rome supported 1500 widows. The church in Antioch supported 3000.[12]

Even though the word "deacons" is not used in this passage, it is obvious that this was the same sort of service as that of deacon, namely, taking care of those who are in need. This ministry becomes a complement to the ministry of the teacher. Just as one finds the titles "overseers" and "elders" later in the epistles, so one finds "deacons" mentioned with them (Phil. 1:1 and 1 Tim. 3:1-13; Knight feels that the mention of *antilempseis,* "helps" in 1 Corinthians 12:28 is a designation of the deacons in Corinth).[13] The ministry was already present. As Peter speaks of gifts, he refers to them falling into two broad, yet distinct categories: teaching and serving (1 Pet. 4:10-11). Likewise, Paul, in his commendation of Timothy and Epaphroditus, portrays two types of ministry in the two men: Timothy was his understudy as a preacher and missionary. Epaphroditus engaged himself in practical service (Phil. 2:19-30).[14]

From the passages which deal with the ministry of deacon, or those others using the term *diakoneo, diakonos,* the following patterns can be learned: First, the deacon has a task of practical service. Acting, rather than speaking, is emphasized. A deacon could certainly have the ability to preach — Stephen and Philip later became two of the most famous preachers of the early church. Both had the gift of evangelism. But the task of being a deacon was not preaching. Likewise, it wasn't ruling. Instead, it was serving. Second, they were assistants to the preachers. The church chose them so that the apostles could be supported and relieved to do the work most crucial to their office. Third, the apostles gave the deacons their job description. Their ministry was dependent upon and subordinate to the ministry of the teachers of God's Word.[15] Fourth, through the ministry of the seven, the murmuring ceased. Thus the ministry of deacon, when rightly exercised, facilitates harmony in the local church, rather than the opposite.

Strauch contrasts the ability of ministering as a deacon with that of being a preacher. The task of a preacher, he notes, requires an ability to communicate the word. The task of a deacon requires an ability in deeds:

> People who are strong in deeds, on the other hand, tend to be administrators, organizers, doers, helpers, supporters, builders, ministers of mercy, and givers. . . The Seven, as a group, were appointed to a ministry of deeds, although, at least two of them were also mighty in word.[16]

Personal Requirements for the Deacon

The ability to fulfill the role of deacon does not depend upon the age or social standing of a Christian. Two passages present the qualifications of deacons: Acts 6:3-6 and 1 Timothy 3:8-13. They will be listed and explained in the following paragraphs.

First, he needs to be one of the church members. "Choose seven men from among you" (Acts 6:3 NIV). A deacon needs to be a man well known by the church, not one that was received into the membership a few weeks earlier.

Second, He needs to be filled with the Holy Spirit (6:3). The fulfillment of this requirement does not come through a particular experience. Rather, it comes through obedience to the Word of God, coupled with a submission to the Spirit's work in the heart. Both in this passage, and in Ephesians 5, the filling of the Holy Spirit is tied together with wisdom. The invisible filling of the Spirit is made visible though the manner of life of the Christian. If a person is living in sin for a time, he is not qualified for the task of deacon.

Andrew Murray understood by experience how the Spirit of God worked mightily in his own and others' lives. Though his spiritual counsel in the following quote was aimed at all regenerate Christians, it is especially applicable to deacons in the requirement of being spirit-filled. Murray states that many Christians

> ... are looking for some great inflow of the Spirit's power to enable them to do mighty works, while they forget that as believers they already have the Spirit of Christ dwelling in them. They forget that more grace is only given to those who are faithful in the little, and that it is only in working that we can be taught by the Spirit how to do the greater works.[17]

Third, he needs to have a good reputation (Acts 6:3; 1 Tim. 3:8). Knight states, "The word σεμνός (*semnos*) when used of a person, means that the person is 'worthy of respect.'"[18] How he handles himself while at work, or in community activities, or among his neighbors is just as important as how he handles himself in the church. In fact, how he acts in pressured situations at work will be the way he handles himself in pressured situations in the church.

Fourth, he has to possess self-discipline (1 Tim. 3:8). This self-discipline is crucial in three areas: 1) He has to be able to control his tongue ("not double-tongued"). Earle notes, "The adjective *dilogos* (only here in the NT) has the idea of saying something twice, with the bad connotation of saying one thing to one person and something else to another."[19] Many matters with which he has to deal are confidential. Spreading them around will cause mistrust in the whole church, and eliminate further chances for ministry. The same goes for a tendency to quickly get into arguments. Not only does this make others uneasy, it frustrates the majority to regularly get bogged down in arguments, instead of getting on with the ministry. 2) He needs to exercise self-control in the area of alcohol. A man who gets drunk is disqualified from this kind of ministry. So is one who likes to go to parties where the alcohol flows freely. The prohibition campaigns of frontier preachers throughout the 19th century in America are typically made fun of in today's society (and even by some Christians). Their efforts, however, saved the American frontier from complete social disaster. 3) He cannot be covetous. The deacon's work often has to do with collecting and distributing money. Only men who can be trusted with money qualify for the ministry.

Fifth, he needs to be one who knows his Bible (1 Tim. 3:9).[20] It has been explained previously that the elder and the deacon are distinguished from one another by the gift of teaching. Nevertheless, the deacon needs to be a man who knows his Bible and the basic doctrines of the faith well. He must to be one who studies regularly. He cannot be a person who will shift his theological position the next time he hears a new preacher. Likewise, he will often be asked questions from church members and outsiders about Bible teachings or church positions. Inability to answer is unimpressive, particularly to unbelievers. The best way for a deacon to receive his theological training is to read his Bible through again and again, and to pay careful attention to the teaching of the Word of God in the church setting. In Ephesians 4:11-16 Paul relates that the teaching ministers of the church have the responsibility for equipping deacons for their ministry.

Sixth, he must be a good family leader (3:12). Life at home displays the genuineness of a man's faith. No children are perfect angels, but a deacon needs to first demonstrate at home that he is leading before he can lead in the church. MacArthur explains well, when he says, "Certainly you don't expect to see complete sainthood in children, but they are to follow their father's faith with a measure of godly conduct."[21] Strauch comments, "Caring for the local church is more like managing a family than managing a business or state. Therefore, a man's ability to manage God's church is directly related to his ability to manage his own household."[22] Though Strauch was speaking of elders, the same holds true for both types of church leaders. A man who cannot control his own children will lack authority when church members need correcting. Gangel sums up the point by saying, "To put it very simply, weak fathers make weak elders or deacons."[23]

Seventh, he needs to be proven (1 Tim. 3:10). A passage of time between the man's conversion and baptism and his election to the office of deacon is an absolute must. This does not mean an officially designated amount of time, or a pre-deacon category. Saucy notes, "The use of the present tense does not suggest a specific test or trial period, but rather the constant observation which would lead to a reputation of proven character and maturity in the Christian life."[24] If a Christian is active in ministry in the church, it will become obvious to most with time whether he is qualified to serve as a deacon. The minimum that is required is that he has a blameless character, and that he is faithful.

Nuttall summarizes,
> Deacons are to be the finest of men. Their standing with God and man must be satisfactory. They are needful to the work. They are the "John the Baptists" of the church. All that you can say about the character and ministry of John is good for the deacon. He must never seek his place in the sun. His humility will cause him to give deference to God's leader and his strength will wield destruction against any politics or power plays. These men are to be respected. The highest honor is due those who serve. Their tender ministry among the saints is a tranquilizing influence. They are the guardians of love and examples of servants.[25]

1 Timothy 3:11 speaks of women, in the context of deacons' qualifications. The passage is somewhat ambiguous because it simply states, "likewise women" (*gynaikas hosautos*). This is interpreted either as "deaconesses" or "wives of deacons." The difficulty in determining the translation is obvious when one examines various translations. The AV, NKJV, and Luther all have, "their wives." The NIV, NEB and NLB all have "their wives," with "or deaconesses" written in the margin. The NASB reads "Women must likewise be dignified." The NRSV translates, "women," then gives the alternatives of "deacons' wives" and "deaconesses" in the margin.

In favor of the meaning of "their wives" is the fact that the word *diakonoi* is not attached here. Second, *gyne,* can mean "wife" as well as "woman." Third, there is no mention of marital fidelity "the wife of one husband."[26] In favor of the meaning "women deacons" is the fact that for "their wives," the definite article (*ton*) before or the genitive pronoun (*heauton*) after *gyne* should be present. Second, it is unusual that the wives of deacons should be given attention, but not the wives of the overseers.[27] Third, in Romans 16:1 Paul refers to Phoebe as the *diakonos* of the church in Cenchrea. That there was an order of female deacons in churches shortly after the death of John is clear from the writing of Pliny the younger, in his *Epistle to Trajan* (X.96). This book takes the position that the New Testament recognizes female deacons, or deaconesses. Their role is limited, however, in that women are not allowed to hold authority over men or to teach a group of men (1 Tim. 2:12).

The Exercise of the Ministry of Deacon

The deacon plays a decisive role in the spread of the Gospel and the growth of the church. Granted, all Christians need to be servants, but the deacon must be one especially. Nuttall states that deacons have both a "temporal and eternal ministry. Their work must not be viewed as secular and it can be understood as organizational only as long as none of their duties are viewed as a contrast with the spiritual."[28] If he does his ministry the right way, it will cost him a lot of time and energy. The main task of the deacon is service. Christ has called him to help others. His fellow Christians need him. The Bible tells us that what a man sows, he will also reap (Gal. 6:7). A deacon who likes to gossip will help develop a gossiping church. A deacon who regularly compromises with the world or is open to false teaching will lead others to do the same. Before he begins his ministry he needs to already be an example of good and faithful Christian living.

Galatians 6:2-5 teaches that Christians need to, at times, carry the burdens of one another. This defines the role of a deacon: he helps others carry their burden. Whenever he visits other church people he should be able to tell quickly what spiritual, physical, or financial needs they have. It goes without saying that Christians bring their problems directly to a pastor, or simply help one another without speaking to a pastor or deacon. There are times, however, when individual Christians cannot do enough to help one in need. A deacon who fulfills his role organizes and motivates other church members in the ministry of helping. Indeed, organization and management of service in the church are a crucial part of the work of deacon. Strauch points out,

> Mismanagement and disorganization ruins families, businesses, governments, and churches. It is the product of the polluted soil of greed, laziness, carelessness, lovelessness, and selfishness. It is not from God. Therefore the family of God should not be

mismanaged. God should receive our best effort, energy, and skill. The entire account of Acts 6 is a sterling example of good organization and loving care for the people of God.[29]

As has already been mentioned, the whole church, from the New Testament perspective is a service organism. Deacons motivate and develop the whole church in doing service. Andrew Murray points out that it is the Lord's intention that every Christian, no matter how feeble, is to serve and evangelize. Deacons can help a great deal in bringing this to pass.[30]

The deacon also has the task of hospitality. Often guest speakers, missionaries, or traveling workers need a place to stay or a meal. This isn't simply the task of the pastor to provide. The deacon needs to do this ministry as well, and to learn how to motivate other church people to perform the same thing. If the deacon's door is open to other members of the church, he can influence them in a very positive way. But he needs to make it clear early in his ministry that his home is not the place for criticizing other members or leaders of the church.

Above all, the deacon needs a burning desire to serve Christ and his church. No amount of reading books, receiving instruction, attending seminars will substitute for the desire to work for God. A deacon needs to see the church as the body of people purchased by the blood of Christ (Eph. 5:2). His labor in serving and helping the people of his church is the same as serving the Lord himself.

Training

For all serious tasks of the church, people need training. This holds true for the ministry of deacon. When deacons are ineffective in the church part of the blame often lies with the church's pastors. Preachers usually define doctrine and Christian living for their congregations well. But they tend to commit deacons to their ministry without instructing them or defining their task. Servants need some understanding of their responsibilities and how to execute them before they will have a chance to become effective.

The primary avenue of training for a deacon is his study of the Word of God, both in private and under the teaching of others. 2 Timothy 2:17 teaches that the preparation for a life of good works is a process which centers around learning the Bible. There are various means of teaching deacons about ministry in addition to regular church Bible teaching times. These include special instructional classes (which need to be interactive, not simply lecture type), seminars or conventions, guest teachers, videos and tapes. But we also learn from other people. In this latter aspect, a deacon can learn by accompanying a pastor in his hospital visitation, or in his visitation of members in their homes, or in personal evangelism. A new deacon can and should learn from older deacons. From older Christians especially he can learn how to avoid controversies. We learn to serve by watching others serve, and by serving with them.

John Mark was probably never a preacher, but simply a servant, a man who accompanied preachers in their travels and helped them. After his first failure, Barnabas took him under his wing and taught him how to minister (Acts 15:39). Toward the end of his life, from prison, Paul wrote to Timothy, "Pick up Mark and bring him with you, for he is useful to me for service" (2 Tim. 4:11). Could there be any higher praise for a Christian than that?

Recommended Resources

Strauch, Alexander. *Minister of Mercy: The New Testament Deacon*. Littleton: Lewis and Roth, 1992. (Strauch does a fair amount of Biblical exposition on the subject.)

Nuttall, Clay. *The Weeping Church*. Schaumberg: Regular Baptist Press, 1982.

Murray, Andrew. *How to Work for God*. Springdale: Whitaker House, 1982. (This book was originally written for pastors and teachers in Christian ministry. The principles laid out are helpful for deacons as well, as the subject is service for the Lord.)

Burge, G.M. "Deacon, Deaconess," *Evangelical Dictionary of Theology*, Walter Elwell, ed. Grand Rapids: Baker, 1984. (A brief and good explanation of the biblical concept of deacon.)

Beyer, Hermann. "διακονέω" *Theological Dictionary of the New Testament*, Vol. II. Geoffrey Bromiley, trans. Grand Rapids: Eerdmans, 1964, 81-93. (The most thorough linguistic and exegetical presentation of the concept of "Ministry, Deacon" of all the works here listed. This is helpful since many churches and church leaders are uncertain of the real meaning and purpose of the role of deacon.)

"Deacon Caring Ministry Seminar" conducted by Dr. Howard Bixby, Church Development Ministries / PO Box 722 / Clarks Summit, PA 18411 / 570-945-0107 (Sat. 9:00-3:30) / hlbixby@juno. com (This is a one-day seminar for pastors and deacons, defining the work of the deacon from the NT perspective and explaining its practical applications. Over the past two decades more than 20,000 pastors and deacons have taken part in the seminar).

Notes

[1] Hermann Beyer, "διακονέω," Theological Dictionary of the New Testament, II. Geoffrey Bromiley, trans. (Grand Rapids: Eerdmans, 1964), 84.

[2] Hans Küng, *The Church,* Ray and Rosaleen Ockenden, trans. (Wellwood: Search Press, 1968), 390.

[3] G.M. Burge, "Deacon, Deaconess," *Evangelical Dictionary of Theology*, Walter Elwell, ed. (Grand Rapids: Baker, 1984), 296.

[4] Henry George Liddel and Robert Scott, *A Greek-English Lexicon* (Oxford: Oxford University, 1968), 398.

[5] Beyer, 91.

[6] Some Christian groups and some individual Christians hold the view that there was no regular membership in the early church. The New Testament shows otherwise. Those baptized on the day of Pentecost were numbered, and added (προστίθημι) to the 120 disciples. In this instance, the word means, "to add, i.e. of persons added to a group already existing." BAGD, 719. In Acts 6, the Christians knew exactly which widows belonged to the church. In 1 Tim. 5:9, widows are enrolled (καταλέγω – BAGD, 413),

[7] Simon J. Kistenmacher, *Acts* NTC (Grand Rapids: Baker, 1990), 220.

[8] BAGD, 885. LSJ does not list this meaning for any occurrence of χρεία in secular Greek (see *LSJ*, 2002-2003).

[9] Spencer argues to the contrary, that the grammar points to the congregation, rather than the apostles, as those who laid hands on the seven. F. Scott Spencer, *The Portrait of Philip in Acts* JSONT (Sheffield: University of Sheffield, 1992), 196.

[10] See the explanation in Chapter 1, page 12. Rabbinic literature calls them, "the seven of the city," or "the best seven of the city." Individually, these men were denoted as "shepherd," or "director." Hermann Strack and Paul Billerbeck, *Kommentar zum Neuen Testament aus Talmud und Midrasch*, Vol. III (Munich: C.H. Beck, 1924), 641-642. Alon calls them "arcons." Gedaliah Alon, *The Jews in their Land in the Talmudic Age*, Gershon Levi, trans (Jerusalem: Magnes Press, 1980), 177-179.

[11] St.Bk., 643.

[12] Kenneth Scott Latourette, *A History of the Expansion of Christianity*, Vol. I (New York: Harper, 1937), 266.

[13] George A.F. Knight, *The Pastoral Epistles* NIGTC (Grand Rapids: Eerdmans, 1992), 176.

[14] Historical evidence outside of the New Testament that the office of deacon was established early in the life of the Church is found in *The Epistle of Clement*, 44.4; Hermas, *Visions* 3.5.1; Ignatius, *Ephesians* 2.1; *Magnesians*, 6.1; 13.; *Trallians* 2.2; 3.1; 7.2; *Polycarp* 6.1.

[15] For some churches, which have several deacons who stay in the church and one pastor who changes every five years, this conclusion sends up a red flag. They envision themselves as having to change their beliefs every five years. The presence of elders who are lay-preachers would certainly eliminate this concern. But there are other measures and safeguards as well. This work does not have the space to go into them.

[16] Alexander Strauch, *Ministers of Mercy: The New Testament Deacon* (Littleton: Lewis and Roth, 1992), 31.

[17] Andrew Murray, *How to Work for God* (Springdale: Whitaker House, 1982), 8.

[18] Knight, 168. Kelly says that the word "at once covers outward temper and inward bearing." J.N.D. Kelly, *The Pastoral Epistles* (Peabody: Hendrickson, 1987 rprn), 81.

[19] Ralph Earle, *1 & 2 Timothy,* EBC (Grand Rapids: Zondervan, 1978), 367.

[20] Bornkamm argues that the phrase, "the mystery of faith," simply means "faith." G. Bornkamm, "μυστήριον," TDNT, IV, 822, as does BAGD, 530. Whereas Ellis, 367, Knight, 169, Kent, 139, Lenski, 596-597, White (EGNT), 115, and Huthner, 123, take it as referring to the revealed Christian truth.

[21] John MacArthur, *The Master's Plan for the Church* (Chicago: Moody, 1991), 88.

[22] Alexander Strauch, *Biblical Eldership* (Littleton, CO: Lewis and Roth, 1986), 81-82.

[23] Kenneth O. Gangel, *Feeding and Leading* (Grand Rapids: Baker, 1996), 11.

[24] Robert Saucy, *The Church in God's Program* (Chicago: Moody, 1972), 158.

[25] Clay Nuttall, *The Weeping Church* (Schaumburg, IL: Regular Baptist Press, 1985), 151.

[26] George W. Knight, 171. Strauch gives a number of reasons why he interprets the 1 Tim. 3:11 passage as "deacon's wives." Strauch, 121-126.

[27] J.N.D. Kelly, *The Pastoral Epistles* (Peabody, MA: Hendrickson, 1987 rprn), 83.

[28] Nuttall, 148.

[29] Strauch, *Ministers of Mercy*, 32.

[30] Murray, 20.

Conclusion

Here is what the New Testament teaches about church government: it has both form and freedom. The local church governs itself. Its only outside authority is Christ. All members take part in church decisions (though many decisions do not concern all of the assembly). This, however, does not eliminate leadership. Rather than being contradictory, the two principles of congregational decision making and strong leadership create a balance in church life. The church must have leaders. She needs Christians who have the courage to make hard decisions. Local church leaders need to be mature Christians, who are led by the Holy Spirit. Church members are obligated to respect their leaders. There are two types of church leaders: pastors (elders, overseers) and deacons. Pastors are chiefly concerned with the ministry of the Word of God and with the oversight of the church. Deacons, on the other hand, are concerned with care, service and the organization of service in the church. They motivate others in the church to serve through their activity and example. This type of leadership corresponds to the example of Christ, since He was both shepherd and servant.

The self-governing church only functions well through the use of the Scriptures. People cannot minister well, or understand roles and limits properly, unless they are a Bible-taught, Bible-reading people. At the same time, church leaders and church members need to deal with one another in grace. Leaders will never be perfect this side of heaven.

One needs to be careful not to overemphasize the teaching of the New Testament about church organization, as if it were the most important thing in Scripture. Above all one would hope that what is written in this book will not be used as a club on some pastor, deacon, or congregation. The local church is not first of all an organization. Among other things, she is the temple of God (1 Cor. 3:16-17). Jesus said that Israel's Temple was meant to be a house of prayer (Mt. 21:13), rather than an assembly hall for commerce, noise and conflict.

In New Testament times there was a temple to the goddess, Artemis, in Ephesus as well as a secular *ekklesia*. On one day all the citizens of the city rushed into the theatre for an assembly (*ekklesia*). Even though they came, as the Bible says, "with one accord," (Acts 19:29), the crowd were full of anger and confusion. Most of the people didn't even know why they were there (19:32). The one thing all understood was to cry out, "Great is Artemis of the Ephesians!" The city clerk had to correct the *ekklesia* and warn them that because of the uproar they had created, they were in danger of being accused before Rome itself (a most serious predicament).

The local church is the temple of God. What the citizens of Ephesus let loose in their secular *ekklesia*, they would never have dared attempt in the temple of Artemis: the temple was a holy place. The citizens of Ephesus could separate their assembly from the holy temple, but God's people can never separate their assembly from God's temple. They are one and the same. Church gatherings, including business sessions, are no place for rancor, politicking, one-uppance, "pulling a fast one," or merchandizing. Each time the church comes together, for whatever purpose, its members enter God's temple and stand in the presence of Christ.

Bibliography

Books

Aland, Kurt, Matthew Black, Carlo M. Martini, Bruce M. Metzger, and Alan Wikgren, eds. *The Greek New Testament*. Stuttgart: United Bible Societies, 1996.

Alon, Gedaliah. *The Jews in their Land in the Talmudic Age*. Gershon Levi, trans. Jerusalem: Magnes Press, 1980.

Arnold, Clinton E. *The Colossian Syncretism*. Grand Rapids: Baker Books, 1996.

Aristotle. *The Politics*. T.A. Sinclair, trans., revised ed. London: Penguin Books, 1981.

Bauer, Walter, F.W. Gingrich, and Frederick Danker. *A Greek-English Lexicon of the New Testament*. Chicago: University of Chicago, 1979.

Barna, George. *Marketing the Church*. Colorado Springs: NavPress, 1988.

Baron, Salo Wittmayer. *A Social and Religious History of the Jews*, Vol. II. New York: Columbia University, 1957.

Bengel, Johann Albrecht. *New Testament Word Studies*, Vol. 1, Charlton Lewis and Marvin L. Vincent, trans. Grand Rapids: Kregel, 1971 rprn.

Boyer, James. *For a World Like Ours: Studies in 1 Corinthians*. Winona Lake: BMH Books, 1971.

Browning, Wilfried. *A Handbook of the Ministry*. London: Mowbray, 1984.

Bruce, F.F. *The English Bible*. New York: Oxford University, 1970.

Burgener, Karsten. *Amt und Abendmahl*. Bremen: Selbstverlag, 1985.

Calvin, John. *Commentaries on the Epistles to Timothy, Titus, and Philemon*, William Pringle, trans. Grand Rapids: Baker, 1989 rprn.

_____. *Institutes of the Christian Religion, II*. Henry Beveridge, trans. Grand Rapids: Eerdmans, 1977 rprn.

Carroll, Peter. *Religion and the Coming American Revolution*. Toronto: Ginn-Blaisdell, 1970.

Carson, D.A, ed. *The Church in the Bible and in the World*. Grand Rapids: Baker, 1987.

Carson, D.A., Douglas J. Moo, and Leon Morris. *An Introduction to the New Testament*. Grand Rapids: Zondervan, 1992.

Catechism of the Catholic Church. New York: Doubleday, 1995.

Clearwaters, Richard C. *The Local Church of the New Testament*. Minneapolis: Central Press, 1954.

Cobb, Sanford H. *The Rise of Religious Liberty in America*. New York: Cooper Square, 1968, rprn.

Couch, Mal, ed. *A Biblical Theology of the Church*. Grand Rapids: Kregel, 1999.

Cowen, Gerald P. *Who Rules the Church: Examining Congregational Leadership and Church Government*. Nashville: Broadman and Holman, 2003.

Dexter, Henry. *Congregationalism*. Boston: Congregational Publishing Society, 1865.

Doellinger, Ignaz. *Beitraege zur Sektengeschichte des Mittelalters*, vol. I. Darmstadt: Wissenschaftliche Buchgesellschaft, 1968, rprn. from 1890 ed.

Dunn, James D.G. *Unity and Diversity in the New Testament*. London: SCM Press, 1984.

Erickson, Millard. *Christian Theology*. Grand Rapids: Baker, 1985.

Estep, William R. *The Anabaptist Story*. Grand Rapids: Eerdmans, 1975.

The Federalist Papers. New York: Modern Library, n.d.

Finzel, Hans. *The Top Ten Mistakes Leaders Make*. Colorado Springs: Cook Communications, 2000.

Friend, W.C.H. *The Rise of Christianity*. Philadelphia: Fortress, 1984.

Edward Gibbon, *The Decline and Fall of the Roman Empire*, Vol. I. New York: Random House, n.d.

Gene Getz. *Elders and Leaders: God's Plan for Leading the Church*. Chicago: Moody, 2003.

_____. *Sharpening the Focus of the Church*. Chicago: Moody, 1986.

Greenwood, John. *A Handbook of the Catholic Faith*. New York: Doubleday, 1956.

Grimm, Herold J. *The Reformation Era: 1500-1650*. New York: Macmillan, 1973.

Hamilton, Alexander, John Jay and James Madison. *The Federalist Papers*. New York: Modern Library, n.d.

Harnack, Adolf von. *Die Mission und Ausbreitung des Christentums*, 4th ed. Wiesbaden: VMA Verlag, 1924.

Hatch, Edwin and Henry A. Redpath. *A Concordance to the Septuagint*, 2nd ed. Grand Rapids: Baker Books, 1998.

Hatch, Nathan O. *The Democratization of American Christianity*. New Haven: Yale University Press, 1989.

Hay, Alexander Rattray. *The New Testament Order for Church and Missionary*. Audubon: New Testament Missionary Union, 1947.

Heimert, Alan. *Religion and the American Mind*. Cambridge, MA: Harvard University, 1966.

Hendricksen, William. *The Gospel of Matthew.* Grand Rapids: Baker, 1973.

Hughes, Philip E. *The Second Epistle to the Corinthians* NIC. Grand Rapids: Eerdmans, 1962.

Jackson, F.J. Foakes and Krisopp Lake. *The Beginnings of Christianity, Part I.* Grand Rapids: Baker, 1965.

Jefferson, Charles. *The Minister as Shepherd.* Hong Kong: Living Books for All, 1973 rprn.

Keener, Craig S. *Paul, Women and Wives.* Peabody, MA: Hendrickson, 1992.

Kelly, J.N.D. *The Pastoral Epistles.* Peabody, MA: Hendrickson, 1987 rprn.

Kennedy, D. James. *Evangelism Explosion.* Wheaton: Tyndale, 1977.

Kent, Homer, Jr. *The Pastoral Epistles.* Chicago: Moody, 1957.

Kistenmaker, Simon. *Acts.* Grand Rapids: Baker, 1990.

Klassen, Walter. *Anabaptism in Outline: Selected Primary Sources.* Scottdale, PA: Herald Press, 1981.

Kober, Manfred E. *The Case for the Singularity of Pastors.* Ankeny: Faith Baptist Bible College, n.d.

Knight, George W. *The Pastoral Epistles* NICNT. Grand Rapids: Eerdmans, 1992.

Knowling, R.J. *The Acts of the Apostles*, EGC, Vol. II. Grand Rapids: Eerdmans, 1979rprn.

Köstenberger, Andreas J., Thomas R. Schreiner, and H.Scott Baldwin, eds. *Women in the Church.* Grand Rapids: Baker, 1995.

Koumoulides, John A, ed. *The Good Idea: Democracy and Ancient Greece.* New

Rochelle: Aristide D. Caratzas, 1995.

Küng, Hans. *The Church*, Ray and Rosaleen Ockenden, trans. London: Search Press, Ltd., 1968.

Lane, William. *Hebrews 9-13* WBC. Nashville: Word, 1991.

Latourette, Kenneth Scott. *A History of the Expansion of Christianity*, Vol. 1. New York: Harper and Brothers, 1937.

Liddel, Henry George and George Scott. *A Greek-English Lexicon*, 9th ed. Oxford: Clarendon, 1968.

Lightfoot, James B. *St. Paul's Epistle to the Philippians*. Grand Rapids: Zondervan, 1953 rprn.

_____. and J.R. Harmer, *The Apostolic Fathers: Greek Texts and English Translations*, 2nd ed. Michael W. Holmes, ed. Grand Rapids: Baker, 1992.

Longenecker, Richard N. *Acts* EBC. Grand Rapids: Zondervan, 1981.

Martin Luthers Ausgewählte Werke, Vol. 3. Munich: Christian Raiser Verlag, 1938.

MacArthur, John Jr. *Answering Key Questions about Elders.* n.p. 1984.

Maxwell, John C. *The 21 Irrefutable Laws of Leadership.* Nashville: Nelson, 1998.

McCune, Rolland. "Systematic Theology III" unpublished notes. Allen Park: Detroit Baptist Seminary, n.d.

McGee, J. Vernon. *Through the Bible with J. Vernon McGee*, IV: *Matthew-Romans* Pasadena: Through the Bible Radio, 1983.

McKenzie, John L. *Authority in the Church.* London: Geoffrey Chapman, 1966.

McLachlan, Douglas. *Reclaiming Authentic Fundamentalism.* Independence: American Association of Christian Schools, 1993.

McLoughlin, William G. *New England Dissent: 1630-1833*, Vol. I&II. Cambridge: Harvard University, 1971.

Meyer, H.A.W. *Commentary on the New Testament*, IV. William P. Dixon, trans. Winona Lake: Alpha Publications, 1979 rprn.

Mickelson, Alvera, ed. *Women, Authority and the Bible*. Downers Grove: InterVarsity, 1986.

Murray, Andrew. *How to Work for Christ*. Springdale: Whitaker House, 1983.

Neander, August. *Geschichte der Pflanzung und Leitung der christlichen Kirche durch die Apostel,* Vol. 1. Gota: Perthes, 1890 rprn.

Nuttall, Clay. *The Weeping Church*. Schaumburg: Regular Baptist Press, 1985.

Owen, John. *The Holy Spirit*. Grand Rapids: Sovereign Grace, 1971 rprn.

Pettegrew, Larry Dean. *The New Covenant Minsitry of the Holy Spirit*. Grand Rapids: Kregel, 2001.

The Works of Philo. E.D. Yonge, trans. Peabody: Hendrickson, 1993.

Piper, John and Wayne Grudem, eds. *Recovering Biblical Manhood and Womanhood: A Response to Evangelical Feminism*. Wheaton: Crossway, 1993.

Radmacher, Earl. *The Nature of the Church*. Hayesville: Schoettle, 1996.

_____. "The Question of Elders." Portland: Western Baptist Press, 1977.

_____. *Salvation*. Nashville: Word, 2000.

_____. "Scripture and Contemporary Varieties of Congregational Government." (Unpublished document, 1987.)

Rainer, Thom S. *The Book of Church Growth: History, Theology, and Principles*. Nashville: Broadman and Holman, 1993.

Ridderbos, Herman. *Paul: An Outline of his Theology.* John Richard De Witt, trans. Grand Rapids: Eerdmans, 1975.

Roberts, Alexander and James Donaldson, eds. *The Ante-Nicene Fathers,* Vol. 5. Peabody: Hendrickson, 1994 rprn.

Robertson, A.T. *A Grammar of the Greek New Testament.* Nashville: Broadman, 1934.

Ryken, Philip Graham. *City on a Hill: Reclaiming the biblical Pattern for the Church in the 21st Century.* Chicago: Moody, 2003.

Sande, Ken. *The Peacemaker,* 2nd ed. Grand Rapids: Baker, 2003

Sanders, J. Oswald. *Spiritual Leadership.* Chicago: Moody, 1980.

Saucy, Robert. *The Church in God's Program.* Chicago: Moody, 1972.

Schaff, David. *History of the Christian Church,* Vol. V. New York: Schribner's, 1907.

Schaff, Philip, ed. *The Creeds of Christendom,* Vol. III. Grand Rapids: Baker, 1990. rprn.

_____. *History of the Christian Church,* Vol. III & IV. (Grand Rapids: Eerdmans, 1974 rprn.

Schirrmacher, Thomas. *Ethik,* Vol. I. Neuhausen: Hännsler, 1994.

Schweizer, Eduard. *Church Order in the New Testament,* Frank Clarke, trans. London: SCM, 1961.

Schurer, Emil. *The History of the Jewish People in the Age of Jesus Christ,* II, revised ed. Geza Vermes, Fergus Millar and Matthew Black, eds. Edinburgh: T & T Clark, 1979.

Snow, Charles M. *Religious Liberty in America.* Washington, DC: Review and Herald, 1914.

Spencer, F. Scott. *The Portrait of Philip in Acts,* JSONT. Sheffield: University of Sheffield, 1992.

Spurgeon, Charles. *Lectures to my Students.* Grand Rapids: Baker, 1977 rprn.

Strack, Hermann and Paul Billerbeck. *Kommentar zum Neuen Testament aus Talmud und Midrasch,* Vol. III. Munich: C.H. Beck, 1924.

Strauch, Alexander. *Biblical Eldership.* Littleton: Lewis and Roth, 1986.

_____. *Biblical Eldership,* Revised edition. Littleton: Lewis and Roth, 1995.

_____. *Minister of Mercy: The New Testament Deacon.* Littleton: Lewis and Roth, 1992.

Streeter, B. H. *The Primitive Church.* New York: Macmillan, 1929.

Stowell, Joseph M. *Shepherding the Church.* Chicago: Moody, 1997.

Sweet, William W. *Religion in the Development of American Culture.* New York: Charles Scribner's Sons, 1952.

Tocqueville, Alexis de. *Democracy in America.* George Lawrence, trans. New York: Harper, 1988.

Turretin, Francois. *Institutes of Elenctic Theology,* Vol. III. James Dennison, Jr., ed. Phillipsburg, NJ: Presbyterian and Reformed, 1997.

Wagner, Charles U. *Laborers Together.* Schaumburg: Regular Baptist Press, 1988.

_____. *The Pastor: His Life and Work.* Schaumburg: Regular Baptist Press, 1976.

Walvoord, John. *The Holy Spirit.* Grand Rapids: Zondervan, 1965.

Westcott, B.F. *The Epistles of St. John.* Grand Rapids: Eerdmans, 1982 rprn.

Wallace, Daniel B. *Greek Grammar Beyond the Basics.* Grand Rapids: Zondervan, 1996.

Articles from Periodicals and Internet Documents

"A Biblical Style of Leadership: Gene Getz debates Larry Richards," *Leadership* (Spring, 1981): 68-78.

Ambaum, Jan. "Die Identität des Priesters," *Communio*, 10 (1981): 421-434.

Callam, Daniel. "Bishops and Presbyters in the Apostolic Fathers," *Studia Patristica*, Vol. XXXI, (1997): 107-111

Campbell, R. Alstair. "The Elders of the Jerusalem Church," *Journal of Theological Studies*, 44 (October, 1993): 511-539.

Campbell, J.Y. "The Origin and Meaning of the Christian Use of the Word ΕΚΚΛΗΣΙΑ" *Journal of Theological Studies* 49 (April, 1948): 130-142.

Comfort, Earl V. "Is the Pulpit a Factor in Church Growth?" *Bibliotheca Sacra* 140.557 (1983): 64-70.

Cornick, David. "The Reformed Elder," *The Expository Times* 98.8 (1987): 235-240.

Decker, Rodney J. "Polity and the Elder Issue," *Grace Theological Journal* 9.2 (Fall, 1988): 257-277.

Delany, Robert G. "A Congregational Church Government Presentation," (internet document) http://www.ifca.org/Voice/02May-Jun/delnay.htm.

Glasscock, Ed. "The Biblical Concept of Elder," *Bibliotheca Sacra* 144 (Jan-Mar, 1987): 244-257.

Houghton, Myron J. "Congregational Rule versus Elder Rule." *Faith Pulpit*. (February, 1986).

Jefford, Clayton N. "Presbyters in the Community of the Didache," *Studia Patristica* Vol. XXI (1989): 124-128.

Knight, George W. "Two Offices: Two Orders of Elder," *Presbyterion* 11 (Spring, 1985): 1-12.

Mappes, David. "The New Testament Elder, Overseer, and Pastor," *Bibliotheca Sacra* 154 (April, 1997): 169-174.

McLachlan, Douglas "Who Makes the Decisions at Your Church?" *Baptist Bulletin* (October, 1998): 12-15.

Nideng, Norman "Stop the Voting: You're Wrecking My Church," *Moody Monthly* (March, 1982): 7-9.

Quinn, Jerome D. "Die Ordination in den Pastorbriefen," *Communio* 10 (1981): 410-420.

Rayburn, Robert. "Three Offices, A Reply to George W. Knight," *Presbyterion* 12 (Fall, 1986): 105-114.

Ratzinger, Joseph Cardinal. "Die kirchliche Lehre vom sacramentum ordinis," *Communio* 10 (1981): 434-445.

"Sharpening the Pastor's Focus: An Interview with Gene Getz." *Leadership* (Summer, 1985):12-19.

Smith, Chuck."Principles of the Calvary Chapel Movement: 2. Church Government." (internet document) http://www.calvarychapel.com/hope/library/smith-chuck/books/ccd/02_church_gov.htm (12/29/03)

Schöllgen, Georg. "Monepiskopat und monarchischer Episkopat: Eine Bemerkung zur Terminologie," *Zeitschrift zum Neuentestamentlischen Wissenschaft* 77, 1-2 (1986): 146-151.

Stedman, Ray C. "A Pastor's Authority." Discovery Papers, No. 3500. Palo Alto: Discovery Publishing, 1976.

"Symposium: The Body Christ Heads," *Christianity Today* 1 (August 15, 1957): 3-13.

Taylor, Larry. "What Calvary Chapel Teaches: Church Government." (internet document) http://www.calvarychapel.com/cheyenne/books/WCTGover.html. (12/29/03)

Wallace, Daniel B. "What it takes to lead the church," (Internet Document) http://www.bible.org/docs/soapbox/leaders.htm. 1/ 29/03.

_____. "Who Should Run the Church? A Case for the Plurality of Elders." (internet document), http://www.bible. org/docs/soapbox/caseform.htm. (10/28/02).

Whitney, Bob. "A Proposal for Elder-Led Church Government," (internet document) http://www.ifca.org/Voice/02May-Jun/ whitney.htm. (12.29.03)

Young, Frances M. "On ΕΠΙΣΚΟΠΟΣ and ΠΡΕΣΒΥΤΕΡΟΣ," *Journal of Theological Studies* 45 (April, 1994):142-148.

Articles from Books, Encyclopedias, Dictionaries, Atlases

"Arnold of Brescia," *Oxford Dictionary of the Christian Church*, 2nd ed. F.L. Cross and E.A. Livingstone, eds. Oxford: Oxford University, 1982: 92.

Beyer, Hermann W. "διακονέω," *Theological Dictionary of the New Testament*, II. Gerhard Kittel, ed. Grand Rapids: Eerdmans, 1965: 81-93.

_____. "ἐπισκέπτομαι, κ.τ.λ." *Theological Dictionary of the New Testament*, II. Gerhard Kittel, ed. Grand Rapids: Eerdmans, 1965: 599-622.

Burge, G.M. "Deacon, Deaconess." *Evangelical Dictionary of Theology*. Walter Elwell, ed. Grand Rapids: Baker, 1984: 295-296.

Chaney, Charles. "The Pastoral Epistles on Care Giving," *Caring for the Harvest Force*. Tom A. Steffen and F. Douglas P. Pennoyer, eds. Pasadena: William Carey Library, 2001.

Cohnen, L. "Bishop, Presbyter, Elder" *New International Dictionary of New Testament Theology*, Vol. I, Colin Brown, ed. Grand Rapids: Zondervan, 1975: 188-201.

MacLeod, D. "Church Government," *New Dictionary of Theology*. Sinclair B. Ferguson and David F. Wright, eds. Downers Grove: InterVarsity, 1988.

Moore, Robert Ian. "Petrus von Bruis," *Theologische Realenzyklopaedie*. Vol. 26 Berlin:de Gruyter, 1996: 486.

"Congregationalism," *The Oxford Dictionary of the Christian Church*, 2nd ed. F.L. Cross and E.A. Livingstone, eds. Oxford: Oxford University Press, 1990: 332-333.

"Democracy, non-Athenian and post-Classical," *The Oxford Classical Dictionary*, 3rd Ed. Simon Hornblower and Antony Spawforth, eds. Oxford: Oxford University, 1996: 453-454.

Hornblower, Simon. "Greece: the History of the Classical Period," *The Oxford History of Greece*. John Boardman, Jasper Griffin, and Oswin Murray, eds. Oxford: Oxford University, 1986: 142-176.

Kirby, Gilbert. "Congregationalism," *New International Dictionary of the Christian Church*, 2nd ed. J.D. Douglas, ed. Grand Rapids: Zondervan, 1978: 251-253.

Lohse, Eduard. "χείρ, χειροτονέω" *Theological Dictionary of the New Testament*, IX. Gerhard Kittel, ed. Grand Rapids: Eerdmans, 1965: 424-437.

Lowndes, Arthur. "Bishop: Anglican View," *International Standard Bible Encyclopedia*, Vol. I. Grand Rapids: Eerdmans, 1939: 479-481.

Lynch, John E. "Church, Church Polity," *The Encyclopedia of Religion*, Vol. 3. Mircea Eliade, ed. New York: Macmillan, 1987: 473-485.

Moore, Robert Ian. "Petrus von Bruis," *Theologische Realenzyklopaedie*, Vol. 26. Berlin: de Gruyter, 1996, 286.

Michel, Otto. "οἰκονόμος," *Theological Dictionary of the New Testament*, V. Gerhard Kittel, ed. Grand Rapids: Eerdmans, 1965: 149-151.

Morris, Leon. "Church Government," *Evangelical Dictionary of Theology*. Walter Elwell, ed. Grand Rapids: Baker, 1984: 238-241.

O'Brien, P.T. "Church," *Dictionary of Paul and His Letters.* Gerald Hawthorne and Ralph Martin, eds. Downers Grove: InterVarsity, 1993: 123-131.

Reike, Bo. "πρέσβυς, κ.τ.λ.," *Theological Dictionary of the New Testament,* VI. Gerhard Kittel, ed. Grand Rapids: Eerdmans, 1965: 651-682.

Saucy, Robert. "Authority in the Church," in *Walvoord: A Tribute*, Donald K. Campbell, ed. Chicago: Moody, 1982

Schmidt, K.L. "ἐκκλησία," *Theological Dictionary of the New Testament,* III, Gerhard Kittel, ed. Grand Rapids: Eerdmans, 1965: 501-536.

Schrage, Wolfgang. "συναγωγή" *Theological Dictionary of the New Testament,* VII. Gerhard Kittel, ed. Grand Rapids: Eerdmans, 1965: 798-841.

Appendix 1
Development of Episcopacy in the First Five Centuries[1]

Period	Sources	Description
1st century	New Testament	Elder-bishops and deacons in each church were under the supervision of the apostles.
Early 2nd century	Ignatius	Elders and bishops were differentiated. Each congregation was governed by bishop, elders, and deacons.
Late 2nd century	Irenaeus Tertullian	Diocesan bishops – a bishop now oversaw a group of congregations in a geographical area; they were thought to be successors of the apostles.
Mid-3rd century	Cyprian	Priesthood and sacrifice. Elders (presbyteros) come to be seen as sacrificing priests. Primacy of bishop of Rome was asserted.
Early 4th century	Council of Nicaea	Metropolitan bishops (archbishops) by virtue of their location in population centers gained ascendancy over chorepiscopi (country bishops).
Late 4th century	Council of Constantinople	Patriarchs. Special honor was given to the bishops of Rome, Alexandria, Antioch, Constantinople, and Jerusalem. Patriarch of Constantinople was given primacy next to the bishop of Rome.
Mid-5th century	Leo I Council of Chalcedon	The supremacy of Rome – Leo I claimed authority over the whole church on the basis of succession from Peter.

[1] Taken from *Chronological and Background Charts of Church History* by Robert C. Walton. © 1986 by The Zondervan Corporation. Used by permission of The Zondervan Corporation.

Appendix 2
Twenty-One Questions
for Spiritual Leaders
from 1 Timothy 3:1-7; Titus 1:5-9[1]

I. God

Not a new convert
1. Can you point to definite areas in your life in which you have spiritually matured during your tour years in seminary?

Devout
2. Does your lifestyle reveal that your highest priority is knowing and walking with God?

II. Yourself

Temperate
3. In the everyday situations of life do you tend to react to them according to a biblical perspective? That is, are you alert to biblical teaching as it bears on your daily living?

Prudent
4. Are you prudent and sober minded to the extent that you can apply biblical principles to walking wisely?

Not quick tempered
5. Do you have a short fuse?

III. Your Family

Husband of one wife
6. Are you totally devoted to your own wife, and not distracted, even mentally, by other women?

One who manages his own household well
7. Do your wife and children love, respect, and obey you and are they responding positively to God?

IV. Others

Hospitable
8. Do you make it your practice to invite to and share your home with both Christians and non-Christian outsiders?

Able to teach
9. Are you able to communicate the Word of God to others in a nonantagonistic manner and able to handle those who disagree with you in a patient and gentle manner?

Appendix 2

Not self-willed
10. Are you able to set aside your own preferences in order to maintain peace with people?

Loving what is good
11. Do you take advantage of opportunities to do good to all men (both Christians & non-Christians) and to build people up rather than tearing them down?

Not a bully
12. Have you overcome the temptation to use the position of leadership to bully people?

Uncontentious
13. Have you developed a dislike for becoming involved in quarrels?

Gentle
14. Are you able to handle other people in a gentle and mild-mannered war?

Just
15. In your relationships with other people are you able to make just decisions; that is, ones which are wise, objective, and honest?

Above reproach
16. Is your lifestyle above reproach when evaluated by those closest to you?

Respectable
17. Do others around you respect you in that your life adorns the Word of God?

Having a good reputation with those on the outside
18. Do you have a good reputation among nonbelievers in the way that you pay your bills, manage your affairs, and react to situations? That is, do they respect you even though they may disagree with your theological viewpoint?

V. Things

Free from the love of money
19. Is the amount of salary you will receive in a position low on your priority list?

Not addicted to wine
20. Are you free from being addicted to anything that might take control of your life and cause a weaker Christian to stumble?

VI. The Bible

Ability to use the Bible
21. Are you able to use the Word of God to exhort people with sound doctrine and to refute those who are antagonistic?

[1] Taken from *Feeding & Leading* by Kenneth O. Gangel. © 2000 by Baker Books, A Division of Baker Book House Co. Used by permission.

Appendix 3
A Partial List of Church Groups in the United States That Practice Local Church Self Government (Congregationalism)

There were three restrictions to the making of this list:

1. It is only partial. When one examines the number of church groups in the United States the amount of research to be done to compile an exhaustive list of those churches practicing congregational rule would require a book in itself. An internet listing of „Church of God,"for example, presents over 50 different groups. Baptists number about 30. This list is presented merely to show that a variety of church groups in the United States practice congregational rule.

2. It is not extended to churches outside of the United States. To do so would require an amount of research and correspondance beyond the scope of this book.

3. Only churches which have Christian trinitarian beliefs are listed.

    The churches here listed either state their policy directly in their literature or their internet websites. In addition some church group headquarters were contacted directly to clarify their position. Some, such as The Nazarene Church and the Weslyian Church, though they have regional superintendents and differing rules regarding holding of property, ordination of ministers, etc., nevertheless affirm a congregational model on the local church level.

    Assemblies of God
    Baptist Churches[1]
    Bible Churches[2]
    The Brethren Church
    Church of God, Anderson, IN
    The Christian Church (Disciples)
    Christian Missionary Alliance Churches[3]

Appendix 3

Church of the Brethren[4]
Church of the Lutheran Brethren
Congregational Christian Churches
Conservative Congregational Christian Conference
Conservative Mennonite Church[5]
Congregational Methodist Church
Disciples of Christ[6]
Evangelical Free Church[7]
Evangelical Mennonite Conference
Evangelical Methodist Church
Grace Brethren Churches
The Mennonite Church
Church of the Nazarene[8]
The Wesleyan Church
United Church of Christ

Notes

[1] Some Baptist churches disavow congregational polity, having adopted instead an elder rule government or another type.

[2] Bible churches actually have various types of church government. One type is congregational rule.

[3] CMA churches have a uniting structure. They affirm rather strongly Congregational polity on the local level.

[4] Local churches are expected to follow denominational programming decided on at the annual conference. Churches are in districts and each district has a moderator. At the local level each congregation chooses its own pastor, holds property and as a group conducts business.

[5] The Conservative Mennonite Church practices a combination of Congregational and Presbyterian Rule.

[6] In addition to the denomination, there are also as many independent Disciples of Christ Churches. Most of these left the denomination in the 1960s.

[7] District Superintendents exercise authority over all churches in their district. Local churches do not ordain their pastors. The Evangelical Free Church makes a strong affirmation of Congregational polity.

[8] The Nazarene and Wesleyan Churches are similar in that local churches hold business meetings in which pastors and other officers are chosen, discipline carried out and property decisions made. All property ultimately belongs to the regional organization. Ordination is authorized by the regional organization.

Motivating Generation X

The Potential of Generation X
as a Challenge for Christians and for Missions

by
Jürg Pfister

I am really praying that many people will read this futuristic, cutting-edge, strategic book. Let's make sure this book gets wide circulation.

George Verwer
Founder of Operation Mobilisation (OM)

Hope and help: such can I best describe the book "Motivating Generation X" by Jürg Pfister. I hope that "Motivating Generation X" will be read by responsible members of congregations and missions boards, that it will be heard and that its corresponding initiatives will be implemented.

Thomas Bucher
President of the Evangelical Alliance of Switzerland

Once I had begun to read Jürg Pfister's book, I could not put it down.

Dr. Roland Werner, Germany

Paperback · 150 pp. · $12,99 / £10,95 / €12,80
ISBN 3-937965-06-8

VTR Publications
vtr@compuserve.com
http://www.vtr-online.de

www.ingramcontent.com/pod-product-compliance
Lightning Source LLC
Chambersburg PA
CBHW032123090426
42743CB00007B/441